WHISTLER

by
Robin Spencer

STUDIO EDITIONS

LONDON

Whistler published 1990 by Studio Editions Ltd.
Princess House, 50 Eastcastle Street
London W1N 7AP, England

ISBN 1 85170 428 0

Printed and bound in Hong Kong

For the memory of James McHugh

INTRODUCTION

In his successful and influential campaign to elevate art above the material considerations of time and place, James Abbott McNeill Whistler did more than anyone to eclipse interest in the larger forces which shape an artist's career. Posterity has shown a limited tolerance of Whistler's cultivation of his own personality, his eccentric appearance, dress and conversation, especially since such details began, soon after his death, to assume a far greater importance than the significance attached to his art. After the Ruskin trial in 1878, or rather because of it, no artist or writer in England or France, except Oscar Wilde, cultivated his personality more assiduously than Whistler. Whether it was the care he gave to the 'white feather' in his hair, a visit to the tailor, the drawing up of a menu, or the preparations for an exhibition, all seemed to occupy his attentions equally, and to fascinate a generation of biographers. He came to maturity as an artist during a period in which there was an insatiable appetite for details such as these. An interview with a journalist, in the artist's studio, home, or in front of his work in a current exhibition, provided as much information about the man and the way he lived as about the art he produced. The widespread dissemination of such information, ultimately through the medium of photography, whether in magazines devoted to art or in the gossip columns of the society papers which proliferated in the 1880s, all fed the needs of a literate public increasingly avid for information about the lives of artists and their activities.

Whistler made the most of these opportunities, and had particular reasons for doing so. The difficulty about an artist's apparently equal involvement in so many unequal pursuits is that the invariable result is divergent opinion about his art. In Whistler's case, the projection of himself as a *flâneur* was compromised at every turn by his diverse activities, which were seen to meet as many social needs as artistic ones. For it is among the artistic fraternity of the social sub-class known as the dandy or *flâneur*, which flourished primarily in Paris, in the wake of Baudelaire, rather than in London, that Whistler's art has so often been considered in relation to the abundance of facts that are known about his life. Victorian London, of which Dickensian images come more readily to mind, rather than the sort associated with the Impressionist vision of Paris, never seemed an appropriate setting for either Whistler or his art. Like Edgar Allan Poe's *Man in the Crowd*, a story prefaced by a quotation from La Bruyère, 'this great misfortune, not being able to be alone', Whistler similarly stood out prominently from the crowd. Instead of looking at life from the wings, as did Degas in Paris, Whistler always occupied centre stage.

Whistler's intention was never to make a literal description of the world, or even to offer the illusion of it, any more than he ever gave a 'true' account of his age or place of birth. He deliberately transformed the subjects of his art as he did his own life. Twice removed from reality, the art he made was not simply an illusion: it became the illusion of artifice. A curtain of mist descends over his subjects and obscures the urban scene which is at one and the same time Victorian London and the landscape from a Japanese print. Factory chimneys in Battersea become *campanili* out of a painting by Canaletto; industrial warehouses are transformed into Venetian palaces in the night. Splashes of brilliant colour obscure a group of Hogarthian figures on a London street. Rembrandtesque shadows engulf a mysterious figure in a doorway. Whistler's art is the very apotheosis of the unspecific, and the very opposite of conventional perception: it is misty, blurred, imprecise, ambiguous – words which are interchangeable as either praise or blame, but totally inappropriate and useless as a scientific record of nature.

Sir Joseph Boehm: Bust of Whistler, *1875, terracotta.*

Whistler substituted visual metaphors derived from art for the prosaic photographic vocabulary practised by so many of his contemporaries. Consequently, his art could evade the new social realities which attracted his French contemporaries, particularly Manet and Degas, in Paris. Paradoxically, the persona he presented to the world was, of necessity, the very opposite of the art which normally might be expected to reflect it. Everything he did or said had to be finely calculated and sharply focused in order to serve and defend his art. By the late 1880s anything connected with Whistler quickly became international 'copy', and was automatically syndicated by the world's press. To meet this need he produced an autobiography, *The Gentle Art of Making Enemies*, in 1890. The quarrels and letters to the press which are contained in it are the very antithesis of the ambiguous or vague. They are relentlessly specific as to time and place; they record opinion, denunciation and disagreement with a world that was practically and metaphorically at odds with the man and his art. Sometimes the literary style is obscure, the language biblical, the expression as outrageous as Carlyle's – to whose Calvinist *angst* he was strongly drawn – but the intention is plain: in the military tradition of West Point, in which he was schooled, attack was always the best form of defence and the only means of survival in the unequal world into which he had been born.

Whistler always prevaricated about his age, but more especially his place of birth, admitting to Boston, Baltimore, or on at least one occasion St Petersburg, but never to the humble cotton-spinning town of Lowell, Massachusetts, where he was in fact born in 1834. There were as many family reasons for him to attend the Military Academy at West Point as there were for him eventually to work as an artist in London. Strong family ties with Britain for more than three generations provided a sound social and economic basis for his finally settling there. His paternal grandfather John Whistler had served in the British army during the War of Independence in 1777; after being taken prisoner he was discharged and became an American. His son, Whistler's father, George Washington Whistler, was born in Fort Wayne, Indiana, then a frontier post, in 1800. Major Whistler, as he became, was a West Point man, with close connections to the Military Academy through his first marriage to Mary Swift. An engineer, he worked on the Baltimore and Ohio Railroads with William Gibbs McNeill, whose sister Anna became his second wife in 1831; he, McNeill and the Baltimore inventor Ross Winans visited England in 1828 to study the railroad system and meet George Stephenson. In order to continue his work as an engineer Major Whistler resigned his commission in 1833, and became, according to the Russians, 'the best railway engineer in the world'. In 1842 he accepted an invitation from Tsar Nicholas I to build the railway from St Petersburg to Moscow. The friendship between Whistler's father and the Winans family, strengthened through his obtaining for their Baltimore factories the colossally lucrative contract of supplying the rolling stock for the Russian project, was cemented when Major Whistler's eldest son George, by his first marriage, married Julia, the daughter of Ross Winans, in 1854. Not only did this bring the two families closer together, but it materially assisted Anna, who after the early death of Major Whistler in 1849 had been left relatively poor. She was then able to call on her elder stepson for financial support.

On the death of his father, George, twelve years James's senior, became head of the family and his guardian. He took an active interest in his half-brother's welfare. When Whistler left for Paris in 1855 George sent him an annual allowance of $350. He continued to assist his career by lending money and buying his pictures, including *The White Girl* (p. 57). Similarly, Ross's son Thomas Winans regularly advanced him money, including $450 for the journey to Europe; in 1858 he bought no less than 35 of Whistler's first set of etchings, *The Twelve Etchings from Nature*, otherwise known as 'The French Set', at two guineas a set. Thus Whistler's statement of 1900 that in Paris he was 'quite a swell' should be set against the countless anecdotes that subsequent biographers cite which suggest his bohemian poverty. Yet not only did the Whistler family always have to practise economies, but it was incumbent on Whistler himself to achieve a degree of financial security, by 1863, when his mother came to live with him in London.

On his mother's side, Whistler's great-grandfather had emigrated to America after the battle of Culloden in 1746. His grandfather Charles McNeill returned to Edinburgh to practise as a doctor and then served with the British Army in the West Indies, settling among relations in Wilmington, North Carolina. It was from this branch of his family that Whistler took pride in his Celtic ancestry, and in his allegiance to the American South. Charles McNeill had two daughters by his first marriage, Whistler's aunts Alicia and Eliza. They had returned to Scotland after the death of their mother, and finally settled in Preston, Lancashire, after Eliza's marriage to William Winstanley. On their journeys between America and Russia Anna and her two boys, James and William, stayed with Whistler's aunts. It was from the Winstanleys' Preston house that Whistler's half-sister Deborah was married in October 1847 to the English surgeon Francis Seymour Haden, who was to play such a prominent and decisive role in Whistler's early professional career in England. It is quite probable that it was through his Lancashire relations that Whistler met other wealthy industrialists in the north-west. Well before he met Frederick Leyland in the mid-1860s Whistler would have

been personally acquainted with the social fabric of bourgeois Lancashire society.

Deborah, the daughter of Major Whistler's first wife, had met the Hadens in Switzerland in the summer of 1847, where she had been sent to recuperate after falling ill in St Petersburg. The Haden family came from Derby and were related by marriage to the Bootts, textile manufacturers and friends of Major Whistler. Thus it was that Deborah made a socially advantageous marriage into a prominent English family, and restrengthened the Whistler family's links with England through a shared heritage of industry and medicine. The immediate family traditions of engineering and medicine were to be furthered on the other side of the Atlantic by James, the artist-inventor, and by his younger brother William, first as a professional soldier in America, and then as a doctor in London.

Major Whistler's ambition was for his son James to become an engineer or architect. In the pioneering spirit of the New World the professional status of engineer was a well respected one, untainted by temptations which, in England, took the form of bribing engineers to deliver favourable technical surveys for Parliament in return for commercial reward. Yet what Major Whistler witnessed in England was nothing compared to the bribery and corruption of the Russian court which dogged the completion of the St Petersburg railway, and contributed to his early death from cholera in April 1849. Even before he reached Russia in 1842, pressure was put on him to persuade the Tsar to continue the railway from Moscow to Odessa. When news of the European revolutions of 1848 reached St Petersburg, the insecure tyranny of Tsar Nicholas's feudal policies precipitated the channelling of funds into the provision of troops in preparation for war. The first casualty to have its funds curtailed was the railroad.

Even before this, in spite of the undoubted favour he enjoyed, Major Whistler met opposition at every turn, particularly from the bourgeois and autocratic members of Russian society who saw the railway as threatening their control over the domestic economy. Although the Major's salary was calculated to be four times that which he had received in America, the Whistlers' years in Russia were neither easy nor financially secure. Major Whistler had three children to support from his first marriage. After James and William (born in 1836), Anna gave birth to three more sons; but between the departure from America and the return from Russia in 1849, all three had died. Furthermore, the luxurious revelry of the Russian court, which for the future of the railway Major Whistler could not altogether ignore, was more or less shunned by Anna's stern Episcopalian faith. Family relations were further strained by Deborah, the apple of her father's eye, but whose youthful high spirits and love of society did not always meet with her puritanical stepmother's approval.

Russia, with its autocratic court and backward feudal system, could not compete with the might of industrialized Europe which was to be the arena for Whistler's art for nearly half a century. Yet it was in St Petersburg that Whistler learnt to speak fluent French, took his first professional instruction in drawing, at the Imperial Academy of Fine Arts, and encountered the work of Hogarth, for which he had a life-long admiration. Although Russia's art was then as backward as its economy, and reliant on an imported version of European academicism, Whistler learnt much from it. His youthful experience of neoclassical orthodoxy, and the place of art in a hierarchical society, found later expression in his confrontation with symbols of authority and power in the highly structured world of Victorian England. The battles he waged against the Royal Academy and the English

bourgeoisie may be seen as a parallel to his father's encounter with the forces of graft and corruption while providing the means for commercial interests to grow fat on the skills and dedication of professional achievement. This was undoubtedly how Whistler saw the early owners of his work, including his own relations – most significantly the Winans side of his family – who in later years resold his paintings at considerable profit to themselves.

His attitude towards the English bourgeoisie is best exemplified by his relationship with his long-standing patron, Frederick Richard Leyland, who owned a Liverpool shipping line and who had commissioned him to decorate the dining room of his London house in 1876. Instead of paying him in guineas – the usual currency for an artist – Leyland had paid only half of what Whistler had asked for the Peacock Room, in pounds, furthermore, the currency of a wage-earning artisan or tradesman whose money is calculated by the time he takes to complete his work. Whistler symbolized himself as the proud peacock, and Leyland as the angry one with silver coins strewn at his feet, in the decoration on the end wall of the Peacock Room. He blamed Leyland because he had no 'business contract' with him over the scheme. After fifteen years of supporting Whistler's art Leyland became his creditor. At the meeting of creditors in June 1879, Sir Thomas Sutherland, Chairman of P & O, and a Whistler collector, presided. Also present were Chelsea tradesmen and solicitors. An impatient builder or baker moved that some explanation be made to the creditors. He was seconded by Leyland. 'At that, Whistler was on his feet, making a speech about plutocrats, men with millions, and what he thought of them . . . With difficulty, solicitor and chairman pulled him down into his seat again.' The strength of these feelings was given pictorial expression in no less than three satirical portraits of Leyland, one of which, *The Gold Scab* (p. 103), shows

The Coast Survey Plate, *1854–5, etching (K.1).*

Leyland as a hideous, tentacled peacock seated, playing the piano, on a model of the White House, Whistler's all-too-briefly occupied house in Chelsea.

When he became famous Whistler received many inducements to return to America, but never did, complaining of its 'vast far-offness'. Post-industrial America would have been anathema to him; he belonged to the period before the Civil War, to the relaxed living and pretended aristocracy of the South, to Baltimore, with its large slave population. There Whistler enjoyed the luxurious living of the Winans family while working on the Coast Survey in Washington immediately prior to his departure for Europe in 1855. This nostalgic vision of a vanishing America Whistler kept alive in London at second hand by reading the stories of Bret Harte and Mark Twain, through which he remained vicariously in touch with his own nationality during his long life as an expatriate.

Given his family's connections and their insecure financial state after the death of his father, West Point was inevitable. He lasted there for just under three years, when he made a calculated departure by deliberately failing chemistry. Late in life he referred to his West Point experience incessantly, seeing in it a metaphor for the military offensive with which he conducted his personal campaign against the 'enemy'. It embodied a code of honour long lost to the polite society of Europe which he lived to see succumbing to modern American money. Through the inevitable dominance of America in world affairs towards the end of his life, he again became its beneficiary, being feted for his fame by rich American collectors such as Vanderbilt, Gardner, Eddy and Freer, all eager to own examples of his art.

In mid-century, Paris provided the training for a career in art, while London supplied the diversity of contacts necessary to live by it. Just as strong as his family's links with Britain was Whistler's exposure to the Victorian art world, which he experienced well in advance of settling in London. In the spring of 1848 he had attended Charles Robert Leslie's lectures on painting at the Royal Academy. Before living in England, Leslie, who had been born in Philadelphia of American parents, had briefly taught drawing at West Point. The following year Whistler was taken by the artist William Boxall to Hampton Court, and that spring visited the Royal Academy to see Boxall's portrait of him. In the same exhibition he would also have seen the first Pre-Raphaelite paintings of Millais and William Holman Hunt to be shown at the Academy. Overseeing all these experiences was Whistler's new brother-in-law, Francis Seymour Haden, a member of the London Etching Club, who counted many friends and acquaintances in London's artistic society, including the Academician John Calcott Horsley, married to Haden's sister Rosamund. Not only did Haden encourage Whistler, but he gave him access to his growing collection of prints, including etchings by Rembrandt, which were to have far-reaching significance for the development of Whistler's graphic art in the years to come. In return, Whistler would dedicate to Haden his first etchings, 'The French Set'.

In Paris Whistler was not easily identified with any one social group. He mixed with the British artists Thomas Armstrong, T.R. Lamont and Edward Poynter, with whom he briefly shared rooms, as well as French artists and musicians. He was much in demand, as he later was in London, for parodies of camp-meeting hymns, negro and French songs:

> . . .there used to be drowning yells and shouts for Whistler, the eccentric Whistler! He used to be seized and stood up on a high stool, where he assumed the most irresistibly comic look, put his glass in his eye, and surveyed the multitude, who only screamed and yelled more. When silence reigned he would begin to sing in the most curious way, suiting the action to the words with his small, thin, sensitive hands. His songs were in *argot* French, imitations of what he had heard in low *cabarets* on the Seine when he was at work there.

He emphasized his origins by wearing white duck and a straw hat of a shape not then known in Europe. He made full use of the American embassy for balls and social occasions, facilities much envied by his British friends. Some of his exploits were undoubtedly bohemian, to the point of parodying Henri Murger's fashionable romantic novel of 1848, *Scènes de la vie Bohème*, which he had probably read before leaving America. Some of his friends later extemporized their reminiscences too freely, and Whistler accused the *Punch* illustrator George Du Maurier of libel for identifying him as Joe Sibley, the 'Idle Apprentice' in the first instalments of the novel *Trilby*, published in 1894. Except for early friendships, his

The Title to the 'French Set', *1858, etching (K.25)*.

association with the English community brought him no discernible artistic nourishment; in his early years Whistler turned for guidance to the Louvre, the art of Rembrandt and eighteenth-century France. For technical instruction he registered as a copyist at the Louvre and worked in the studio of Charles Gleyre. There he would have the same encouragement to work out of doors which Gleyre gave to Monet and Cézanne in the following decade.

Whistler's introduction to modern French art through a chance encounter in the Louvre with Henri Fantin-Latour towards the end of 1858 was the beginning of a more committed attitude, and marked the change from being only a casual bohemian to becoming a serious one. The art of Gustave Courbet, and the encouragement he gave to Whistler, proved a decisive influence during his stay in Paris. In May 1859 he praised Whistler's *At the Piano*, which had been refused by the Salon and instead shown in the studio of the realist artist François Bonvin, along with Fantin's portrait of his two sisters, rejected that year. Like Courbet, whom he quickly came to idolize, Whistler could call himself not only a democrat but a true republican. Courbet's 'negation of the ideal' and his rejection of the historical and imaginary subjects Whistler would have encountered at Gleyre's, in favour of the marginal and rejected characters of empire society as suitable subjects for art, occurred at a time when Paris was rapidly changing under Napoleon III's expansive domestic policies. Since he had no lasting commitment to the orthodox neo-classical tradition of European art, Whistler was soon susceptible to realist subjects and styles. The tour he made down the Rhine in the summer of 1858 was a well-trodden journey for artists, but instead of depicting the landscape in a conventional picturesque manner, he deliberately sought out vernacular architecture and peasant figures. In Paris he added them to a stock of etchings of *métiers*, flower- and mustard-sellers and rag-pickers, who were either swiftly disappearing from view or had already been displaced as a result of Baron Haussmann's plans for radical urban renewal. Deliberately tempered by the well-judged inclusion of two portraits of his brother-in-law's prosperous-looking children, Arthur and Annie, his first set, *Twelve Etchings after Nature*, was published in London at Christmas 1858.

The French artist friends he made in 1858, Fantin-Latour and Alphonse Legros, also at the outset of their careers, to whom he showed his recent etchings, were no less committed to realism than was Whistler. Degas, another friend, described the work of Whistler, Fantin and himself as being 'on the road from Holland', because of their mutual interest in seventeenth-century Dutch painting, which had a marked influence on the work of all three artists at about this time. In the immediate years, both Fantin and Legros were to benefit materially from the contacts Whistler had already made for himself in

Street at Saverne, *1858, etching (K.19 iv).*

London. Together they made up the 'Society of Three', which was dedicated to furthering their professional careers in Paris and London, by keeping each other informed of potential buyers for their work and of other developments in the expanding world of art helpful to their interests. At Whistler's request Haden invited Fantin to visit London in 1859. He returned in 1861 and again in 1864, having met the English lawyer-artist and collector Edwin Edwards, who became a life-long patron.

In return, Fantin's major contribution was as publicist for the Society. He achieved this most notably at the Salon of 1864 when he showed *Homage to Delacroix*, in which Whistler's portrait was the most prominent of all among realist painters and writers, including Manet and Baudelaire. Legros, too, quickly experienced a steady demand for his work in England, sharing with Whistler and Fantin commissions from a Greek family, the Ionides, whose sons, Luke and Aleco, Whistler had met in Paris. As well as purchasing Whistler's first works, Haden also bought those of Legros: one of these, *The Angelus*, a major peasant subject, had attracted the attention of Baudelaire at the Salon of 1859, the same exhibition which had rejected the submissions of both Whistler and Fantin. Legros' reception in London was so favourable that he settled there in 1863, eventually becoming an influential teacher at the Slade School of Art.

From the circle of academicians and collectors centred on Edwin Edwards's comfortable home at Sunbury-on-Thames, and that of the Hadens in Sloane Street, Whistler freely moved to the opposite extreme when, in 1860, he was, according to Du Maurier, 'working hard and in secret down in Rotherhithe, among a beastly set of cads and every possible annoyance and misery, doing one of the greatest *chefs d'oeuvres* – no difficulty discourages him'. He took lodgings in the East End to be near his subjects, and immersed himself in the atmosphere of the river, to the detriment of his own safety and health. He lived in a little inn, rather rough, frequented by skippers and bargees, close to Wapping steam-boat pier. Occasionally he would get stranded in the mud, or else cut off by the tide. So dedicated was he to the project that he caught rheumatic fever, and for a time some of his friends though he might die. The reason for his presence amid the London wharves and docks was twofold: to make etchings of the dilapidated dockside buildings on the Thames as a follow-up to the 'French Set'; and to find authentic Courbet-like realism for a 'subject picture' which would go down well in Paris – he still hoped to have his paintings accepted by the Salon, which had rejected *At the Piano* the previous year. At the same time he needed to prepare a major work for the Royal Academy in order to establish a reputation in England.

During his first years in London he travelled widely in search of new subjects. In the autumn of 1861 he was in Brittany, where he painted a seascape in the manner of the shore-life scenes then currently fashionable in England. The following year he was in south-west France, attempting to paint an even more ambitious seascape, with fisherfolk, rocks, and a rough sea, executed entirely out of doors in a manner that would have appealed to Courbet. In the end the sea was so rough that not only was he nearly drowned, but the technical difficulties inherent in working out of doors on such a scale proved to be a practical impossibility, and the project was never realized. At the same time he wanted to be the first artist of the circle in France, which by this time included Manet, to visit Madrid, see the work of Velázquez and bring back photographs of his pictures to Paris. He got no further than Fuenterrabia on the Spanish border. Another reason for visiting Spain was to find a Spanish genre subject which might be suitable for either London or Paris, because the theme of Spanish peasant subjects was a popular one on both sides of the Channel. Furthermore, his first public success in London, *At the Piano*, which included portraits of Deborah Haden and her daughter Annie, was compared by critics to Velázquez, and had been bought by an English artist, John Phillip, who specialized in Spanish subject-matter.

The public outcome of all these activities turned out to be entirely different from the way Whistler planned it. The large figure picture, begun in Wapping but intended for Paris, was seriously delayed, and eventually shown in London. Instead Whistler achieved national attention in France at the *Salon des Refusés* of 1863 with a picture painted in Paris the previous year, but originally submitted to the Royal Academy, which had refused it. This was *Symphony in White, No. 1: The White Girl* (p. 57), which showed a girl dressed in white, with a soulful expression and dishevelled hair, standing on a bearskin rug with summer flowers strewn at her feet. Critics in London, where the picture was shown in a dealer's gallery in the summer of 1862, as well as in Paris the following year, were anxious to find a meaning for the picture, since Whistler had intentionally left the girl's identity as well as her marital status open to question. In fact the picture was a portrait of Joanna Hiffernan, a red-haired Irish girl of humble origin, whom Whistler had met in London in 1860, and who was to remain his mistress for six or seven years. It is possible that she bore Whistler a child. Although not at all out of place among Whistler's artist friends, particularly Courbet, Jo was to precipitate domestic difficulties for Whistler when he assumed that she could cross the same social divisions in London society that he did. These difficulties were compounded by the arrival of his mother in London in 1863.

The *succès de scandale* which *The White Girl* enjoyed at the *Salon des Refusés* encouraged Whistler to keep in touch with developments in Paris, which he was able to do through his friendship with Fantin. In spite of a negative opinion of his etchings in Paris, the Salon public was reminded of his name by the exhibition of Fantin's group portraits. Following the *Homage to Delacroix* of 1864, in which Whistler tried to persuade his new friend Rossetti to appear, his portrait was again prominent in the Salon the following year when Fantin exhibited *Homage to Truth: The Toast*. This included a similar cast of realist writers and artists, shown in the allegorical company of a nude female figure symbolizing Truth. By making an effort to be represented in all these manifestations Whistler was as much at home in Paris as he was in London. More than at any other period in his career he then seemed to resemble the authentic Baudelairean dandy or *flâneur*. The American artist George Boughton remembered him in the early 1860s with a 'cool suit of linen duck and his jaunty straw hat', making a flying trip to Paris, when he was 'flush of money and lovely in attire'.

Whistler first met Dante Gabriel Rossetti, the founder member of the Pre-Raphaelite Brotherhood, in the summer of 1862. Soon after he met the poet Swinburne, and in March the following year he was in Paris and introduced Swinburne to Manet. Swinburne had been the first English author to write an article on Baudelaire's *Fleurs du Mal*, and in London was much in demand as the composer of original verse to accompany the pictures of his artist friends, as Baudelaire had done for Manet in Paris. He readily supplied poetry for both Burne-Jones and Whistler, for whose *Symphony in White, No. 2: The Little White Girl* (p. 61) he composed the sonnet 'Before the Mirror' in 1864. The concept of synaesthesia, the expression of one sense impression through the medium of another, which Whistler publicly announced when his *Symphony in White, No. 3* (p. 69) was exhibited at the Academy in 1867, originated with romantic art theory in France. It was given specific currency in Baudelaire's verse, and in his writings on Delacroix.

In the 1860s, the art practised by Whistler and his English friends Rossetti and Burne-Jones was directed at a small but growing market. This had been skilfully identified by William Morris, whose firm, Morris, Marshall, Faulkner and Company, supplied artists' designs for textiles, furniture and stained glass, following the encouragement given by the Prince Consort after the Great Exhibition of 1851. Under the practical guidance

Whistler photographed by Etienne Carjat in Paris, c.1864.

of Sir Henry Cole at the South Kensington Museum, who aimed at a unified system of art education, new standards of industrial and domestic design were gradually established in Britain. From the start Whistler had been friendly with architects and designers, in particular Edward Godwin, who shared his interest in Japanese prints, and Thomas Jeckyll, who was no less affected by the cult for Japonisme. Jeckyll later designed the dining room of Leyland's London house, where in 1876 Whistler created the Peacock Room. Also among Whistler's friends was the Cole family, Sir Henry, his son Alan, and their circle from the South Kensington Museum, for which Whistler was asked to supply a wall decoration and later to paint Sir Henry's portrait.

His reputation as an interior designer rested on the work he did in his second house in Chelsea, where in 1867 he decorated the dining room in blue, with a darker blue dado and doors, and purple Japanese fans tacked on the walls and ceiling. The drawing room was painted in flesh-colour, pale yellow and white; on the walls of the hallway was a great ship with spreading sails. Later the dado of hall and stairway was covered with gold and sprinkled with rose and white chrysanthemum petals. From these last designs was developed the concept for the Peacock Room. A similar project may have been proposed to the banker W.C. Alexander, the buyer of Whistler's first nocturne, for rooms in his house at Campden Hill. Whistler's colour schemes were far less costly to make than William Morris's hand-printed textiles and wallpapers, which were labour-intensive to produce and supply. Once the colours had been mixed by Whistler they could be cheaply applied by house painters. Like Morris's schemes, which suited pictures by Burne-Jones, Whistler designed an appropriate colour scheme to enhance his own paintings; it was not, however, until the 1880s that he had the chance to carry out unified wall decorations for his friends.

In the 1860s he was not short of buyers of his work. These included the Ionides family, and other Greek collectors in London such as the Cavafys and Spartalis, whose daughter Christine was the subject of one of Whistler's first essays in the fashionable taste for Japonisme in England, *Rose and Silver: The Princess from the Land of Porcelain* (p. 65). His work was bought by James Leathart, the director of a Newcastle lead-mining works, who owned an important collection of modern pictures; and by William Graham, the Scots MP, who also collected Pre-Raphaelite paintings and was a close friend of

Burne-Jones. From about 1864 there was Frederick Leyland, also a collector of Rossetti and Burne-Jones, who commissioned major figure pictures from Whistler, and later portraits of himself and his family. With members of Leyland's family he became a close friend, regularly visiting Speke Hall, the Elizabethan mansion outside Liverpool which Leyland bought in 1867. In his relationships with all these collectors Rossetti was instrumental in either bringing about an introduction, or else in promoting Whistler's work through the medium of his art-critic brother, William Michael, in whose writing Whistler's name frequently appeared. By late 1863 Whistler had become so friendly with 'the Rossetti lot' that Du Maurier could describe them all as being as 'thick as thieves'.

Although Whistler's paintings and etchings were seen regularly enough in the large exhibitions in London and Paris to warrant critical notice and a steady flow of buyers for his work, the reception it received in public was not always complimentary. This proved especially contentious in relation to the etchings of his brother-in-law, Francis Seymour Haden. Relationships with Haden were strained by the critical recognition given to his etchings in Paris, in preference to Whistler's own, with which the French critic Philippe Burty, writing in the *Gazette des Beaux Arts*, found fault; he even mis-spelt Whistler's name. Whistler and Haden had originally planned to publish a joint portfolio of Thames etchings, with Whistler supplying the downstream low-life subjects, and Haden the upstream rural reaches of the river; but their rivalry put an end to the project. Ironically, while Whistler had pioneered the revival of etching as an artistic medium in Paris, and already broken new ground both in terms of subject matter and style, it was Haden, not Whistler, who

Speke Hall No. 1, *1870, etching and drypoint.*

was involved in the *Société des Aquafortistes* in Paris, and founded the Society of Painter-Etchers in London in 1880, in which Whistler took no part. Their relationship ended in blows in 1867, when Whistler accused Haden of being casual and inhumane over the obsequies he arranged for his medical assistant, a friend of the Whistler brothers, who had died suddenly in Paris. The affair had serious consequences for Whistler, since by this time Haden wielded considerable influence in London society. Through his agency Whistler was forced to resign from the Burlington Fine Arts Club, a social and exhibiting society, membership of which was mandatory for young artists aspiring to become Associates of the Academy, and the necessary passport for an artist's professional career in London.

After 1867 Whistler exhibited at the Academy on only two subsequent occasions, and was obliged, therefore, to seek a public outlet for his work through other channels. For the Salon in Paris the question of nationality offered him a double opportunity, since he was an American national, resident in England. In 1867, for example, he exhibited in the American section of the *Exposition Universelle*, since he had good reason to believe that, as an English juror that year, Haden would have prevented his work from being shown in the English section of the exhibition. As it was, his seascapes were dominated by the American Hudson River school of landscape painting and received little notice. In 1889 he moved his work from the American to the English section, in the belief, mistaken though it proved to be, that he would be given more generous space for it.

Between the death of Delacroix in 1863 and that of Ingres in 1867, Whistler, in his correspondence with Fantin, reviewed the practical and theoretical problems which accompanied the production of realist art. Whistler's overriding desire had been to paint *en plein air*, but he found such difficulty in practice, and such critical unpopularity for it, that after 1865 he attempted it less and less. The writings of Baudelaire, who had praised Whistler's etchings in 1862, and the teachings of Charles Blanc, who had also written about Delacroix, conspired to persuade him to concentrate on the formal qualities of line and colour, and to reassess the realism of Courbet. Courbet's reputation as a radical force among younger artists had declined, especially in 1866, when he accepted a medal from the government. The death of Ingres in 1867 also provided a forum for reassessing neo-classicism and its relation to Delacroix's romanticism, the two ideological and stylistic polarities that had previously divided artists and artistic expression in France. Whistler did not consider Ingres's paintings to be at all Greek, but rather thought of them as being 'viciously French', which was clearly a quality he would like to have been able to claim for his own art.

To exhibit such a 'foreign' style in the Academy, however, where 'classical' French art was rarely seen, would not have been possible. The nearest approximation to it was achieved by Frederick Leighton, who exhibited classically-inspired subject-matter in the 1860s; and by Albert Moore, whom Whistler knew by 1865, and whose art for the next five years much influenced his own. By 1864 he was quarrelling with Legros concerning money, but their rivalry also manifested itself in Paris, where Legros spread stories about the ambitions of Whistler and Fantin to become 'leaders of the new school of art', with the intention of sowing enmity between them and discrediting the friendship they both shared with Manet. In London, Haden used Legros' testimony against Whistler in his campaign to have him expelled from the Burlington Fine Art Club. Accordingly, Legros was dropped from the 'Society of Three', in favour of Albert Moore. Whistler planned a picture, showing Fantin, Moore and himself, in his studio, with Jo as *The White Girl* and a female Japanese figure, a composition he intended to paint life-size for the *Salon*. He also wrote to Fantin of the three of them continuing the 'true traditions of nineteenth-century art'. By 1867 he had disavowed the strong influence Courbet's

The Peacock Room, *1876–7: central shutter, east wall; oil and gold leaf on wood.*

painting had made on his own, and expressed a wish that he had been a pupil of Ingres. By stressing these attitudes he indicated a preference for a non-narrative art with a strong emphasis on colour and line.

Whistler had often been accused by critics, in his 'Japanese' paintings, of being nothing more than a copyist of Japanese prints. Such an accusation was levelled at *The Princess from the Land of Porcelain* (p. 65) when it was shown at the Salon in 1865. Since the accusation of excessive realism was also directed at the work of Fantin's friends, particularly that of Manet, Whistler developed a hybrid style of painting which combined elements from the tradition of Western classicism with the decorative character of Japanese art. The subjects in the set known as the *Six Projects* which he prepared for Leyland were loosely based on Japanese designs after Kiyonaga, but they are unspecific as to time and space, and utilize a series of pre-selected colour harmonies to effect narrative coherence. He clearly hoped that Leyland would commission all six on an enlarged scale, either for Speke or for the town house he acquired in London in 1869. Instead, the only comparable commission Leyland gave at this time was for a set of the *Seasons* from Burne-Jones which, ironically, hung in the dining room at Princes Gate before Whistler transformed it into the Peacock Room in 1876. Leyland did, however, select one of his designs for enlargement, the subject of three girls on a garden balcony (p. 71). The commission dragged on into the 1870s – at least two versions are recorded – but Whistler was never able to complete the composition to his satisfaction, and it became one of the claims Leyland made on Whistler at the time of his bankruptcy in 1879.

So concerned was Whistler with the new direction his art was taking in the late 1860s – to Fantin he referred to 'two years of artistic education' he had given himself – that in 1869 he took rooms in Great Russell Street, in

Bloomsbury, in order to devote himself exclusively to the problem of the 'Three Girls' composition, with no thought of being represented at the Academy until he had achieved a solution to his technical problems. He appealed to Thomas Winans of Baltimore to lend him money so that he could repay Leyland the advance on the project he was unable to resolve. In addition, he still had an unfinished picture on his hands which had been begun as early as 1864, and which at one time he had intended to enlarge to life-size for the Salon. The subject of this was a balcony, overlooking the industrial Battersea shore of the Thames, with robed Japanese figures in the foreground similar to those of the *Six Projects* (p. 73). The unfamiliar combination of realism and imagination, based on a study of classical forms and Japanese prints, provoked an uneasy critical response when it was finally exhibited at the Royal Academy in 1870.

Whistler lived and worked at some thirteen different addresses in Chelsea during a period which spanned more than forty years. His places of residence exactly mirror his economic circumstances at any one point in his career. By deciding to build his own house in Tite Street in 1877, and asking Godwin to design it, Whistler himself directly contributed to a new kind of social mobility in that part of London in the 1880s. In choosing Chelsea as a place to live he was influenced by its cheapness, in relation to the other parts of West London, like Kensington, where his more successful artist contemporaries – Millais and Leighton, for example – could later afford to build expensive homes. Through Rossetti's solicitor, James Anderson Rose, he obtained a lease on 7 Lindsey Row, immediately upstream of Battersea Bridge, early in 1863, moving to No. 2 in 1867 where he lived for ten years. Only once, before his brief occupancy of the White

House, did he made a serious attempt, in 1870, to buy a house, Merton Villa, previously occupied by the large family of the Scottish sculptor John Birnie Philip, which included Beatrice, later Godwin's wife. Even after he could have afforded to, he always chose to lease studios and apartments. Some rooms in his various abodes usually had an unlived-in look to them, with packing cases strewn about. He told the writer Gérard Harry, when in 1890 he visited Whistler at 21 Cheyne Walk, close to where Rossetti had lived: 'You see, I do not care for definitely settling down anywhere. Where there is no more space for improvement, or dreaming about improvement, where mystery is in perfect shape, it is *finis* – the end – death. There is no hope, nor outlook left.'

Chelsea was still essentially a rural village, but the marshes of the Battersea shore opposite were fringed with processing plants for agriculture, and all manner of heavy and light industry. Maltsters and mills, dye and chemical factories, the Morgan Crucible Company and Price's Candle Works were clustered round the spire of St Mary's Church. Overlooking this landscape and connected to it by Battersea Bridge, built in 1771 and resembling the bridges of Edo in prints by Hiroshige, was Chelsea, centred on the tower of the Old Church from which radiated red brick houses of the seventeenth and eighteenth centuries. To the west of Lindsey Row was Cremorne Gardens, illuminated at night by thousands of coloured lights, and offering all manner of entertainments, including dancing and firework displays. It would be closed in 1877 for the building of houses to meet the needs of the rapidly expanding parish. Here, in the same decade that the Impressionists painted the new café society of modern Paris, Whistler represented the nearest equivalent that London could produce. The Thames Embankment at Chelsea was the last section of the river to be embanked; by 1858 it had only reached the west end of Royal Hospital Gardens. It was not until 1874 that it reached Battersea Bridge, and even then it stopped short of Lindsey Row, depriving the residents of its greatest contribution to modern life in Victorian London, an efficient system for sewage disposal to reduce the risk of cholera from the polluted river. The dramatically wide embankment, faced in granite and cast iron, was the nearest resemblance London could offer to the centre of modern Paris. It provided Whistler with a viewpoint for the nocturnes of the river Thames he painted in the 1870s.

At the same time that he pursued work which attracted only a small circle of followers in London, Whistler also found that the nocturnes, harmonies and arrangements he was beginning to paint met with little appreciation in Paris. Artist friends, such as Fantin, disapproved of what they were unable to understand, as much as Fantin disliked the recent work of Manet and the *plein-air* Impressionists whose work was then beginning to be shown in public. Nevertheless, by exhibiting the nocturnes in minor commercial galleries in London, he found a small public, but one appreciative enough to buy them. He also leased, for a year, a gallery in Pall Mall, which he re-decorated in an original fashion with pale-coloured walls, in order to show his portraits of the Leylands and other recent work and thus attract a wider audience for his art.

To extend this circle further he held Sunday 'breakfasts' at the Lindsey Row house, with a menu partly French, partly American, consisting of buckwheat cakes, green corn, and brilliant talk. The conversation ranged from Japanese art to Velázquez, Balzac, Hugo, and recitations from the writings of Bret Harte and Mark Twain's jingles, of which he always had an endless stock. He designed the invitation cards and menus, arranged the table with flowers, blue and white china, and a Japanese bowl of goldfish. Later, Whistler described himself as having 'never dined alone for years', and the print dealer Percy Thomas regarded him as 'a man who could never bear to be alone'. The guests usually included the Coles from the South Kensington Museum and artists such as Tissot and Moore, as well as journalists and critics, including Tom Taylor and Frederick Wedmore. George Boughton recalled the breakfasts as being 'as original as himself or his work, and equally memorable'. Inevitably, gossip afterwards was as much about the man as about his pictures, which, Whistler considered, Taylor and Wedmore treated with little more than amused or tolerant condescension. Their difficulty, of course, was that they found the art as culturally foreign to them as they did the man. Critics such as these were unable to identify poetic sentiments with which they were unfamiliar, and remained unsure of Whistler's intentions in respect of them. Thus Philip Gilbert Hamerton, writing of Whistler's etchings in 1868, was reduced to complaining that his art was 'rarely affecting, because we can so seldom believe that the artist himself has been affected'. However penetrating, sensitive or original Whistler's idiosyncratic observations of nature were considered to be, qualities such as these could not compensate English critics for the strong element of personal detachment with which they sensed he approached his subjects. Reluctant to engage in discussing the reason for this, they invariably concluded that technical inadequacy alone accounted for Whistler's failure, either to provide a 'correct' representation of nature, or else to depict it with sufficient 'poetry' to meet the requirements of conventional art.

This sense of personal detachment is most apparent in the nocturnes. Whistler used every conceivable means at his disposal to distance the viewer from the swiftly changing urban realities of nineteenth-century London. Mist and the reflection of lights on the water assume a

The Velvet Dress, *1873, etching and drypoint (K.105 v).*

greater presence than solid objects, and distance is as ambiguous as in a Japanese print by Hiroshige, on which Whistler based his conception. The indistinct outline of the Battersea shore, its chimneys and spire, the attenuated wooden pier of Battersea Bridge: all are insufficiently described to be easily identified at a glance. A prose transcription of Whistler's art can do no justice to its intent. In thanking Leyland for supplying the name 'nocturne', rather than the more prosaic 'moonlight' (under which title they were first exhibited in 1872), he emphasized his detachment, not only from the content of his art, but also from any further desire to supply a meaning for it: 'You have no idea what an irritation it proves to the critics, and consequent pleasure to me; besides it is really so charming, and does so poetically say all I want to say and *no more* than I wish.' By issuing this disclaimer, which after 1878 he made in various published statements, expressing disdain for the subject-matter of his art, Whistler explicitly asserted the primacy of the artist's imagination, and, implicitly, his right to use any technical means at his disposal to effect it.

In refusing in his art to conform to the verisimilitude of nature, on which so many of his contemporaries relied, Whistler relinquished a degree of control over its interpretation. When cross-examined at the Ruskin trial about *Nocturne in Blue and Silver* (*sic*; p. 83) he stated it was 'not my intention simply to make a copy of Battersea Bridge', but had to concede: 'As to what the picture represents, that depends upon who looks at it. To some persons it may represent all that I intended; to others it may represent nothing.' Nowhere was this discrepancy between form and content more marked than in his portraiture, the primary function of providing a likeness being considered by his critics to be secondary to their formal design. When the Attorney General, for Ruskin, asked Whistler why he called

'Mr Irving an arrangement in black', the judge elicited laughter in the courtroom by observing, 'It is the picture, and not Mr Irving, that is the arrangement.'

Whistler's means to a livelihood depended on an entirely different source from an artist such as Frith, whose large income came from the extensive sale of engravings after his pictures. Instead of seeking mass circulation for his work, Whistler's etchings were aimed at a small group of discerning collectors, who were conscious of the fact that they were issued only in small numbers. In the 1880s and 1890s they became progressively rarer, with Whistler at least supervising, if not printing them all himself, and attending to all aspects of their presentation. Nevertheless, market forces naturally dictated printmaking as the most obvious source of quickly realizable income, to which he always turned when funds were low, especially in the late 1870s. To redress his swiftly diminishing resources he published, through the printselling firm of Henry Graves, mezzotint engravings after his best-known portraits, his *Mother* and *Carlyle* (pp. 81, 85). Whistler's commercial relationship with professional dealers in the 1870s was confined to Graves and Co., which advanced money in return for unsold works they retained until such time that Whistler could redeem them: in the case of the *Mother* and *Carlyle* this was not until 1888 and 1891 respectively. Because Whistler only rarely consigned his work to dealers in the first half of his career he was unable to test the potential resale value of his art, and had therefore to turn again and again to the same patrons, particularly Leyland, to support him. It was in order to increase the outlet for his production that he employed the services of the colourful entrepreneur and one-time secretary to Ruskin, the Portuguese Charles Augustus Howell, who, Whistler later said, 'helped Watts to sell his pictures and raise the prices ... he introduced everybody to everybody, then entangled everybody with everybody else, and it was easier to get involved with Howell than to get rid of him.'

Since most English critics in the 1870s were incapable of critically enhancing an understanding of Whistler's art other than through satire, the currency of its artistic value was measured by the market which supported it. That this was largely a liberal bourgeois one can be gathered from Whistler's remarks to Alan Cole in 1875, when he announced that his 'much blaguarded masterpiece', *Nocturne: Grey and Gold – Westminster Bridge* (p. 91), had been sold to the Honourable Percy Wyndham, 'for the price named in the catalogue . . . So you see this vicious art of butterfly flippancy is, in spite of the honest efforts of Tom Taylor [the art critic of *The Times*], doing its poisonous work and even attacking the heart of the aristocracy as well as undermining the working classes.' The price of 200 guineas which Whistler had already received for several of his nocturnes would have been relatively inconsequential had it not been for Ruskin's criticism of *Nocturne in Black and Gold: The Falling Rocket* (p. 97), exhibited in the newly opened Grosvenor Gallery in the summer of 1877, and there also priced at 200 guineas. Ruskin's criticism, published in his own periodical *Fors Clavigera* for July 1877, and addressed to the 'Workmen and Labourers of Great Britain', stated:

For Mr. Whistler's own sake, no less than for the protection of the purchaser, Sir Coutts Lindsay ought not to have admitted works into the Gallery in which the ill-educated conceit of the artist so nearly approached the aspect of wilful imposture. I have seen, and heard, much of Cockney impudence before now; but never expected to hear a coxcomb ask two hundred guineas for flinging a pot of paint in the public's face.

Applying the standards for art which he had defined thirty years before in defending Turner against his critics, namely that the relative value of pictures should depend on the 'clearness and justice of the ideas they contained and conveyed', Ruskin found Whistler's subject of fireworks in a night sky, painted in an Impressionist manner, to be singularly lacking. In the belief that the duty of the art critic was 'to distinguish the Artist's work from the Upholsterer's', Ruskin explained to his lawyers that 'confusion between art and manufacture' had 'degraded the produce even of distinguished genius into hastily marketable commodities'; and that 'in flourishing periods whether of trade or art the dignity of operative merchant and artist was held alike to consist in giving good value for money and a fair day's work for a fair day's wages'. In writing of Whistler as 'ill-educated' and 'conceited' Ruskin cited a want of education in giving his pictures musical titles, believing that the accusation of a 'pot of paint' was an accurate description of a method that was 'calculated to draw attention chiefly by its impertinence'.

Had the case, when it came to court in November 1878, turned on a serious critique of the *laissez-faire* economics of the Victorian art world, the roles of Whistler and Ruskin as the respective forces of progression and reaction in the history of art might well have been reversed. But Ruskin, who had suffered a mental breakdown the previous year, was too ill to attend and defend his views. In claiming £1,000 from Ruskin Whistler cited the damage Ruskin's criticism had done to his professional reputation, which was indisputably a controversial one. Since the attack he had been prevented from selling his work at anything like its previous price. Although dealers and the keepers of public collections, including the director of the National Gallery, the curators of the British Museum print-room and the Royal Library at Windsor – both of which owned large collections of Whistler's etchings – were subpoenaed to testify to this, none came forward to do so. Inevitably, the trial centred on the technical merits of the paintings, which Burne-Jones, appearing for Ruskin, claimed were sketch-like and unfinished; the implication was that, as an artist, Whistler should be judged incompetent and his work unworthy of consideration as serious art. For Whistler, Albert Moore, William Michael Rossetti and the playwright William Gorman Wills put the opposite view. Frith, and Tom Taylor, found no difference between the nocturnes and 'delicately tinted wallpaper', a popular prejudice then concerning the respective status of art and decoration, but an ironic one, since the market for 'home improvements' had been much influenced by Ruskin's ideas. Furthermore, the buyers of William Morris's products constituted essentially the same market that bought works from Burne-Jones as well as from Whistler. Although Ruskin's words were clearly libellous, it was not easy for Whistler's counsel to show that they were so extreme as to have been activated by malice. Ruskin's counsel needed only to show that Ruskin's words were directed at Whistler's professional claims as an artist, and to question his judgement in asking what the critic sincerely believed to be an extravagant price for a picture which had been voluntarily submitted for critical scrutiny in a public place. Whistler's decision to debate the issue in front of a jury which had neither a commercial nor a professional interest in the outcome inevitably led to the satirical airing of popular prejudices about art, while the verdict for Whistler and the award of a farthing's damages – and no costs – brought satisfaction to neither side. Whistler became bankrupt and Ruskin resigned his Professorship at Oxford.

The Beggars, Venice, *1880, etching and drypoint (K.194 viii).*

In the longer term the trial was of value to Whistler, since he was able publicly to question the value of art criticism, and the role of the art critic as society's method of determining the relative merits of artists. His claim at the trial that 'none but an artist can be a competent critic', reiterated in his first brown-paper-covered pamphlet *Art and Art Critics: Whistler versus Ruskin*, published immediately afterwards, was put into practice on his return from Venice. He would assume for himself the role of the artist as critic. In the shorter term, however, the costs of the trial, and the crippling expense of the White House, as well as the failure of Leyland, now estranged, to support him, made bankruptcy certain. The situation was further complicated in February 1879 by the birth of a second daughter to Maud Franklin, who had been his principal model and mistress since the early 1870s. In order to stave off the inevitable he devised various schemes, with the practical assistance of Charles Augustus Howell, which included the marketing of etchings and the publishing of engravings. Among these plans was the possibility of an advance of £1,000 on a portrait of Disraeli, but it never materialized. By early 1879 Whistler was in desperate financial straits. An auction sale of his possessions was held, bailiffs entered the White House – which was sold to the critic Harry Quilter, a Ruskin supporter – and on 8 May he was declared bankrupt.

The Fine Art Society had already taken more than a passing interest in the fortunes of Ruskin and Whistler. The gallery had invited Ruskin to arrange an exhibition of Turner's watercolours in February 1878 which received immense acclaim and public interest. In addition to exhibiting Ruskin's own drawings they had also opened a public subscription account to defray his costs in the libel action. Shrewdly aware of the public interest which would be generated by an exhibition of Whistler's vision of Venice – a city much in the news then because of Ruskin's campaign to preserve its architecture – the gallery commissioned Whistler to make twelve etchings of the city. For some years Whistler had planned to visit Venice, and the Fine Art Society's offer of £150 for twelve etchings enabled him to go for three months. The society's option to buy the plates for £700 on his return offered a timely opportunity to recoup his fortunes, and to

leave London at a particularly inauspicious moment in his career. The gallery expected Whistler to be back in London early in 1880.

Whistler arrived in Venice with his mistress Maud Franklin, and later moved in with a group of American students which included Otto Bacher. In return for

The Little Lagoon, Venice, *1880, etching (K.186 ii).*

hospitality and particularly the use of the printing press Bacher had brought with him from Germany, Whistler imparted unstintingly his unsurpassed knowledge and mastery of the technique of etching, details of which Bacher later set down in his book *With Whistler in Venice*. The work Whistler planned in Venice was intended as a visual riposte to the critical perception of his shortcomings as a draughtsman, and in particular what he believed would be Ruskin's criticism of his inability to draw architecture. In order to test his own veracity, Otto Bacher remembers Whistler often asking him questions about the progress of his work, so that he could be sure he was describing it rightly to other eyes. 'Tell me', he said to Bacher about the etching *San Biagio*, 'what you see under the large open arch? What figures do you see around the boat? What do you find in the balcony? Do you see the clothes hanging out?' In another etching, *The Doorway*, he asked Bacher if he knew what the objects were which hung from the ceiling of the room glimpsed through the door, and was pleased that Bacher recognized them as being rush-bottomed chairs. In the end he greatly exceeded his commission, producing over 50 etchings.

Whistler's approach to his subjects was very different from that of previous artist visitors to Venice. He generally avoided the large picturesque vistas framed by the grand canals, favouring instead nooks and crannies, courtyards and corners that were off-limits to the typical tourist. In staying much longer than the Fine Art Society expected him to, he was also able to complete 90 pastels which he described to the Fine Art Society's managing director as 'so new in Art that everybody's mouth will I feel pretty soon water'. In the pastels Whistler combined intensely contrasting harmonies of brilliant colour over black charcoal on brown paper, often using the most minimal descriptive language.

Palaces, Venice, *1880, etching and drypoint (K.187 iii).*

When he eventually did return to London in November 1880 he had recourse to several strategies. The first was to capitalize on the publicity which had been engendered by the Ruskin case. This he achieved by two public exhibitions held at the Fine Art Society, in 1880 and 1881, of the Venice etchings and pastels respectively, as well as a third, larger, exhibition of the etchings held in the same gallery in 1883. For the exhibition of pastels Whistler decorated the gallery with a low skirting of yellow-gold, a high dado of dull yellow-green cloth, and a moulding of green-gold, with a frieze and ceiling of pale reddish brown. The pastels themselves, priced on average at 30 guineas each, sold faster than the etchings; and Maud Franklin described how they quickly became 'the fashion': 'All the London world was at the private view – princesses, painters beauties actors – everybody – in fact at one moment of the day it was impossible to move – the room was crammed.' For the exhibition in 1883 Whistler designed the gallery as an 'Arrangement in White and Yellow'. The walls, to a height of about ten feet, were lined with white felt, the skirting and cornice was of a bright canary; there were yellow velveteen curtains, yellow serge settees, yellow matting on the floor, white and yellow chairs, and yellow vases with one yellow marguerite in each. The etchings were framed in white.

Perhaps more significant than either the composition of the guest list for the private view, which was headed by the Prince and Princess of Wales, or the decoration of the gallery itself, was the catalogue Whistler had published to accompany the exhibition. Titled *Mr Whistler and His Critics*, it included past criticism of his art, which was usually adverse, but fragmented and taken from its original context. It was thus made to appear absurd and as ill-conceived as the slightest work of art Whistler had ever been considered guilty of. It offered him the opportunity

Photograph of Whistler painting in his Fulham Road studio, 1884/8. The portrait in the background is probably of Maud Franklin.

of getting his own back on the critics, as when he misquoted Frederick Wedmore for having written of Whistler's etchings in 1879, 'they have a merit of their own, and I do not wish to understand it', instead of 'understate it'. When Wedmore complained, Whistler had the last word by confessing his 'carelessness' in *The World*, warning 'that with Mr Wedmore, as with his brethren, it is always a matter of understating, and not at all one of understanding'. Using this method he was able to make the press work for, rather than against him.

The power of the press, a medium of mechanical reproduction, was not only sufficient to create and undo reputations, it was also the instrument which brought the public, each paying one shilling, into Whistler's exhibitions at the Fine Art Society, regardless of the number of works he sold. Proceeds from the sale of the catalogue, also priced at one shilling, went to Whistler. The more the exhibition was written about the larger was the attendance; the more celebrated the guests, such as the Prince and Princess of Wales, who held back everybody else at the private view, the more column inches would appear in the society journals and newspapers the next day. The dealers fully collaborated in the strategy, just as they encouraged Whistler to set a relatively high price on his work, safe in the knowledge that they stood to receive between 20 and 30 per cent of the value of each work sold. It was essentially because Whistler found this arrangement with the Fine Art Society unacceptable that he turned to Walter Dowdeswell, who mounted two major exhibitions of his work, in 1884 and 1886.

By not shirking the popular verdict of the press – in 1883 Oscar Wilde said, 'Popularity is the only insult that has not yet been offered to Mr Whistler' – Whistler created a new critical forum for English art, which the large exhibition of French Impressionism held at Dowdeswell's later that year was to enhance further. In the

1880s Whistler was regularly referred to as an Impressionist. Critics were therefore obliged to question how he achieved his pictorial effects, however insubstantial they might appear. By choosing a wave, a pretty girl, or a shop front, painted on a tiny panel some nine inches by five, and mounted in an elaborate gold frame as large as the picture itself, Whistler drew attention away from the minimal nature of his subject-matter, and focused it on the method of execution instead. 'An admirer asked the price of a pastel, and when told, exclaimed: "Sixty guineas! That's enormous!" Whistler heard . . . "Ha ha! Enormous! why not at all! I can assure you it took me quite half an hour to draw it!"'

On the assumption that the value he placed on his work was consistent with the claim he made at the trial, that he asked two hundred guineas not for two days' work, but the knowledge of a lifetime, it was also natural that interest in Whistler himself became as great as it was for the art which he made. That interest was expressed in the early 1880s through the medium of his friendship with Oscar Wilde, and broadcast in the columns of *Truth* and *The World*, which published their sparkling repartee. The difference between their use of language was characterized by Arthur Symons:

He [Whistler] was a great wit, really spontaneous, so far as what is intellectual can ever be spontaneous. His wit was not, as with Oscar Wilde, a brilliant sudden gymnastic, with words in which the phrase itself was always worth more than what it said; it was a wit of ideas, in which the thing said was at least on the level of the way of saying it.

In the early 1880s Oscar Wilde became the focus of 'Aesthetic' society in London. In 1882 he was invited by Richard D'Oyly Carte's American representative to give a series of lectures to coincide with the comic opera *Patience*, then playing in New York. The main comic creation of Gilbert and Sullivan's opera, a satire on contemporary aestheticism, was the 'fleshly' poet Bunthorne, a compound of Whistler, Wilde, and the easily caricatured aspects of 'taste' associated with the Grosvenor Gallery, where Whistler was still a regular exhibitor. As the opera's publicist, as well as, in part, its subject, Wilde gave lectures in America on 'The English Renaissance of Art', and on 'House Decoration', in which his debt to Ruskin, Morris, and Whistler was abundantly clear. He upheld the South Kensington Museum as the ideal place for the student of handicrafts, and the Peacock Room as an example of decorative purity. Wilde and Whistler lived only doors apart, in Tite Street, Chelsea; and it is obvious that, for the purpose of his American tour and a lecture he gave to the Royal Academy students in 1883, Wilde greatly benefited from regular meetings with Whistler.

The aesthetic foibles which George Du Maurier cartooned in *Punch*, satirizing Whistler's painting among other things, Wilde made fashionably acceptable to the class which aspired to an interest in art, house decoration and dress reform. Whistler's previous position as detached artist, outside society, thus became compromised at being accepted into it by Wilde's all-embracing aesthetic doctrines. Whistler had already acknowledged society by painting the portraits of, among others, Lady Meux, the wife of a prominent London brewer, and Lady Archibald Campbell, a member of the Scottish aristocracy. His sitters included the *nouveaux* upper middle class, and those aspiring to it, which Wilde represented on the stage and to which his proselytizing on behalf of modern art was intended to appeal. In order that he should not, once again, become either the victim of the *littérateur*, or the creation of the critic, Whistler asserted personal control over his presence in society, in order to retain within it his artistic independence. As his landscapes and seascapes became smaller in size, and their existence approached invisibility, so his own physical presence grew in contrasting visibility to his art. He wore, at this time, a black or fawn frock coat, white trousers, patent leather shoes, a top hat with a straight French brim, and carried a cane of ever-increasing length.

The more publicly this posturing became identified with Wilde's, however, the more pressing became Whistler's need to distance himself from it. His answer was the 'Ten O'Clock' lecture, given in the Princes Hall on 20 February 1885. In it he dissociated himself from the Aesthetic Movement, the art that had become 'a sort of common topic for the tea-table', 'to be coaxed into company, as a proof of culture and refinement'. The lecture proscribed 'false prophets', such as Ruskin and Morris, and art critics; but above all, derided the fashionable aesthetic climate for art as a moral force, in which Wilde, parodying Ruskin, had invited the bourgeois to participate. In the decade of nascent socialism in England, Whistler unfashionably surprised his liberal audience by lifting 'from their shoulders this incubus of Art'. He offered an attitude to art which was anti-materialist, rather than a fresh interpretation of art's relationship to society. He sought to deny that an 'artistic period' had ever existed, but that the artist had always been a man who stood apart 'in relation to the moment at which he occurs – a moment of isolation – hinting at sadness – having no part in the progress of his fellow-men'. Here Whistler reclaimed the ground first trodden by Poe and Baudelaire.

The brilliant Impressionist prose of the lecture was derived from the language of French Romanticism; the examples he gave to support his claim – Rembrandt's Jewish subjects, Velázquez' 'inaesthetic' crinolines, a decorated fan by Hokusai, and the Parthenon sculpture – were intended to reflect the experience of modernism through the great art of the past, which both Whistler and Manet had achieved in their work. In calling the Impressionists, Manet, Monet, Renoir and Whistler, the *avant-garde*, Théodore Duret, in his book of that title published the same year, implied how advanced their art was compared to that of their contemporaries. By including chapters on Wagner, Japanese art, Reynolds and Gainsborough, as well as on the philosophers Schopenhauer and Herbert Spencer, he also emphasized, like Whistler, that great art was evolutionary, and was created irrespective of nation, century or medium. So Whistler, in his lecture, asserted the primacy of the artist who is 'born to pick and choose, and group with science . . . that the result may be beautiful – as the musician gathers his notes, and forms his chords, until he bring forth from chaos glorious harmony'; and scorned, like Baudelaire, the limitation of Nature which 'seldom succeeds in producing a picture'. In the mistaken belief that the language of 'poetic symbolism' – a 'lofty' mountain, a 'vast' lake, an 'infinite' ocean – was appropriate for painting, the art critic looked 'with disdain, upon what he holds as "mere execution" . . . So that, as he goes on with his translation from canvas to paper, the work becomes his own', and 'the *painter's* poetry is quite lost to him'.

In acknowledging Whistler to be merely a 'master of painting', rather than an artist, Wilde, in his review of the lecture, denied Whistler his claim to be the best judge of art, reserving that right for the poet, to whom he gave the status of 'supreme artist'. The recognition Whistler sought as an artist, coequal with the distinction accorded a poet, was granted him not in England but in France, in the Symbolist milieu of Stéphane Mallarmé, who translated the 'Ten O'Clock' lecture in 1888.

Portrait of Mallarmé, No. 1, 1894, lithograph (W.66) (detail).

As aesthetic amanuensis to Whistler in Paris – where he moved to a house in the Rue du Bac in 1892 – Mallarmé was able to elevate the discourse of art far above 'a common topic for the tea-table'. Together, they worked to distance art from the 'disastrous effect' it had had 'upon the middle classes' in London, where Wilde had 'brought the very name of the beautiful into disrepute'. In London, the 'eccentricity' of Whistler's personal appearance had been negatively equated with a similar perception of his art as eccentric; in Paris one was considered the natural product of the other, as this description of Whistler's attraction for Mallarmé by their mutual friend, the Symbolist poet Henri de Régnier, suggests:

> Mallarmé instantly succumbed to Whistler's magic and was touched, as though by a conjuror's wand, by the ebony cane which this great dandy of painting

wielded so elegantly. Everything in Whistler justified the curiosity and affection Mallarmé felt for him: his mysterious and pondered art, full of subtle practices and complicated formulae, the singularity of his person, the intelligent tension in his face, the lock of white hair amid the black, the diabolical monocle restraining his frowning brows, his prompt wit in the face of the scathing retorts and cruel ripostes, that ready and incisive wit which was his weapon of defence and attack.

To Mallarmé, Whistler was like Edgar Allan Poe, a social outcast but for his art, susceptible to comfort from it alone; after the death of his wife it would become his one source of human solace on earth. He treated it as 'a goddess of dainty thought', who, nonetheless, was capable when roused of treachery, and even of defeating her creator. On a small portrait of the New York dealer Edward Kennedy, Whistler worked away all afternoon, 'hissing to himself' in the garden of the Rue du Bac, one summer day in 1893. 'If Kennedy shifted – there were no rests – Whistler would scream, and he worked on, and on, and the sun went down . . . a paint rag came out – and, with one fierce dash, it was all rubbed off. "Oh, well", was all he said.' If, after a day's unsatisfactory work he could not trust himself to efface it, he might ask someone else, perhaps Walter Sickert, to return to his studio and destroy it for him. There was always the 'rubbing out and despair'; his reluctance to part with a portrait, for the sake of 'just two touches' that eluded him; the abandoning of a picture, or the continuation of one only from the clothes, outgrown by their first owner, but worn by successive models, long after the original sitter had despaired of receiving his portrait.

Subjects of all ages, from all periods of Whistler's career as a portraitist, testify to the relentless sessions he imposed on them. His mother posed standing for two or three days, until she grew tired; little Cicely Alexander 'often finished the day in tears'. Comte Robert de Montesquiou, the model for Des Esseintes in Huysmans's *A Rebours*, and Proust's Baron Charlus, told the De Goncourts of having to pose more than a hundred times, when he felt that Whistler, 'drawing his life from him with the fixity of his attention, was sucking something of his individuality from him'. He was finally so drained that he had to be revived by 'a wine made with coca, which helped him recover from these terrible sittings'. For Whistler 'Industry in Art' was 'a necessity – not a virtue – and any evidence of the same, in the production, is a blemish, not a quality; a proof, not of achievement, but of absolutely insufficient work, for work alone will efface the footsteps of work'. The concentrated pain communicated by the artist to his canvas and sitter was never illusory, but always real. Henri de Régnier remembered the burns on Mallarmé's legs, the result of sitting for too long near the fireplace when he posed for Whistler's lithograph of him. There was more to Whistler's art than what he called 'the coloured photograph kind of thing'.

The welcome reception by the Parisian *littérateur* of Whistler's art, to which the Anglo-Saxon critics had previously been so hostile, was made doubly ironic by the stinging review which his friend of a quarter of a century, the poet Algernon Charles Swinburne, gave the 'Ten O'Clock' lecture in 1888. By dissecting the argument with pedantic literalism he tried to show that Whistler was neither qualified to write about art, nor logically justified by the theories he put forward in support of his own painting. Although in the end forgiving, Whistler was deeply offended. In denouncing Swinburne as '"outside" – Putney', he implied how out of touch he had become with modern French literature, with the heritage of

Baudelaire's verse he had championed 26 years before, and with Mallarmé, to whom in 1876 he had addressed his poem *Nocturne*, written in French.

Whereas Whistler's work was generally seen in a negative light in England, because it did not embody the storytelling principles which critics were so used to applying to narrative art, it was given a quite different reception in Europe, where Whistler exhibited widely from 1882. Large collections of his art were shown in Munich in 1888 and 1889, at the Paris Salons, in the galleries of Georges Petit in 1883 and 1887, and Durand-Ruel in 1888. In 1889 a large exhibition of his oils, watercolours and pastels was shown in America for the first time, at Wunderlich's gallery in New York. By 1883, when the portrait of his mother, *Arrangement in Grey and Black* (p. 81), was awarded a third-class medal at the Salon, and 1884, when he exhibited for the first time with the *Société des XX* in Brussels, Whistler was becoming an established figure in the pantheon of international modernism. By the mid-1880s, especially in Paris and Brussels, the affairs and reputations of artists were being ordered more and more by artists themselves, in collaboration with critics sympathetic to their aims. Whistler benefited from exhibiting with a younger generation, in the European exhibiting societies of the 1880s and 1890s, after being relatively overlooked abroad in the 1870s when all his energies were absorbed by his work for Leyland and the battle with Ruskin.

Whistler believed that his argument with Ruskin had been between the brush and the pen, and that he had fought it on behalf of all artists whose careers could be made or broken by the power of the printed word. While he never forgot this lesson, he also remembered his experience with Leyland, and in his lifetime witnessed the control of art passing, in part, from the patron to the artist. When, as President of the Society of British Artists in 1886, he was challenged by a dissatisfied member who declared that 'the patrons' would decide whether they found Whistler's 'half-uncovered' walls of the gallery preferable to seeing the work of 'many artists of more than average merit' which had been rejected, he retorted, 'Now it will be for the patrons to decide absolutely nothing . . . Indeed, the period of the patron has utterly passed away, and the painter takes his place – to point out what he knows to be consistent with the demands of his art – without deference to patrons or prejudice to party.'

In his renewed campaign to seek artistic independence, if not in England then abroad, he had the support of Théodore Duret, who had been introduced to him by Manet. Duret wrote influentially about Whistler in the *Gazette des Beaux Arts*, and also reviewed, clearly at Whistler's behest, the Grosvenor Gallery exhibitions of the early 1880s. Thus Whistler re-emerged, after an interval of some 15 years, as a major figure on the Parisian art scene, in the decade when Impressionism was giving way to Symbolism as the *avant-garde* in French art. Consequently, his painting was especially conducive to the work of French writers such as J.K. Huysmans and Gustave Geffroy, and those influenced by Mallarmé, who did not seek Impressionism's scientific description of nature, but instead preferred an art that evoked it through suggestion and visual metaphor. Accordingly, Huysmans described the nocturnes as 'dream landscapes' which transport the observer 'on magic carpets into times that have never been, regions that never were, suspended worlds, far from modern life, far from everything'. Whereas English critics were usually able to relate Whistler's art to that of Manet and the Impressionists, in the 1880s it was with Puvis de Chavannes and the Symbolists that his flat, dark canvases were more often compared by

critics in France. Later, British writers, such as R.A.M. Stevenson, D.S. MacColl and George Moore, the exponents of the 'New Art Criticism', who were schooled in Baudelaire rather than Ruskin, took their cue from their French colleagues by making an aesthetic virtue out of Whistler's minimalism, as when Moore in 1893 described the nocturne owned by Duret as 'purple above and below, a shadow in the middle of the picture – a little less and there would be nothing.'

Photograph of Whistler and Mortimer Menpes, c.1885.

Whistler provided the major focus in London for those younger artists who were aware of the significance of the new artistic developments in Paris. By 1884 he had gathered a group of 'Followers', the most serious of which were Walter Richard Sickert and Mortimer Menpes. These two accompanied him to St Ives, Cornwall, in the winter of 1883–4, where they painted seascapes on small wood panels in a *plein-air* Impressionist style informed by Whistler's tonal manner. Combining these lessons with their experience of recent French art, the 'Followers' experimented with every new style, from Degas's and Gauguin's to Seurat's and Pointillism, which had emerged in Paris by the end of the decade. Resolutely opposed to all literal descriptions of nature, and adopting as their manifesto the aesthetic principles of the 'Ten O'Clock', they found their subject-matter in the music halls and streets of London, adopting unusual viewpoints, and often using, like Whistler, the most minimal expressive means. Variations on these styles were practised by what Whistler called the 'Steery-Starry-Stotty lot', meaning Philip Wilson Steer, Sidney Starr and William Stott of Oldham, all of whom became members of the Society of British Artists, and were known as English Impressionists when they later held exhibitions at the New English Art Club.

With membership of the Royal Academy closed to him, the chance of being elected as a member of the Society of British Artists in 1884 offered Whistler a platform to increase the opportunities for young English artists. The S.B.A., one of the oldest exhibiting societies in London, had by the 1880s become little more than an alternative market-place to the Academy; its walls were hung with saleable productions by artists adhering to well-worn, indeed outmoded subjects and styles. Whistler immediately took an immense interest in the society's affairs; so much so, that by June 1886 he had been

Walter Sickert, *1895, lithograph (W.79).*

elected its president. The reforms he introduced meant a severe reduction in the number of pictures shown, in order to exclude mediocre work. He also attempted to pass a resolution which prohibited members of the Hanging Committee holding official positions in other bodies, such as the Royal Academy. This offended those artists who wished to use their influence to increase their sales in both places. It was Whistler's objection to the S.B.A. remaining 'a shop', rather than his ambition for it as an 'art centre', in line with continental practice, which so offended insular English tastes. Inevitably, he favoured

Sheet of drypoints of Whistler by Mortimer Menpes, c.1885.

the work of the 'Followers', and those working in Impressionist styles, such as Ludovici, whose art, like Sickert's, was much influenced by Degas. By inviting foreign artists to exhibit – in 1887 Claude Monet came to London and showed four paintings – he demonstrated his indifference to any significance attached to nationality in art. In 1886 he wrote, 'You might as well talk of English Mathematics. Art is Art, and Mathematics is Mathema-

tics.' What others called English art, he believed to be 'not Art at all, but produce, of which there is, and always has been, and always will be, a plenty . . . They are the commercial travellers of Art, whose works are their wares, and whose exchange is the Academy'.

Under Whistler the S.B.A. was given a new lease of life. Instead of elaborately patterned wallpaper he introduced plain walls of different shades, and redesigned the catalogues and invitation cards. In 1887, Jubilee year, he obtained royal patronage for the society by submitting to Queen Victoria a specially designed portfolio of his etchings of the Naval Review. So successful was Whistler's presidency that a knighthood was seriously rumoured in the press. But the experiment, however successful it was judged artistically, was commercially short-lived. The *haute bourgeoisie* and the *demi-monde* were not always present in the right combination at the private views to ensure enough sales, and the finances of the S.B.A. began to decline. Whistler was forced to resign in June 1888, and while 25 artists resigned with him, 'the British', Whistler quipped, 'remained'.

Whistler made a distinction in his art, between the formal portraits of high bourgeois subjects exhibited at the Salon, which he thought would appeal to the public, and what he called artists' pictures, which he sent to smaller galleries to attract the interest of his fellow painters. In one letter to Duret of 1882, he significantly asked him to take Manet to see the portrait of Lady Meux, then on exhibition at the Salon. Artists, especially Manet, whose art was the very embodiment of Baudelairean *vie moderne*, would have appreciated the less formal 'artists'' pictures, for which Maud Franklin was usually the model, dressed in the latest Parisian or London fashion, on which, in 1881, she told Otto Bacher, she had just spent one hundred pounds.

The difference between the two kinds of portrait, the

high bourgeois and the *demi-monde*, had other implications for Whistler during the years in which he described himself as having 'no private life'. Maud, who clearly came from humble stock, was not always accepted, by the rules of Victorian society, as a suitable partner for Whistler in public, in spite of the fact that she appears to have accompanied him whenever she could. She exhibited under the name 'Clifton Lin' at the Grosvenor Gallery, and then at the S.B.A. as a 'pupil of Whistler'; so did Beatrice Godwin, the architect's widow, under the name of 'Rix Birnie'. The transfer of Whistler's affections from one to the other was the source of considerable tension. Maud, who by 1885 had two, if not three children fathered by Whistler, continued to call herself 'Mrs Whistler' in public even after he married Beatrice. The conflict was first made public by the presence in the 1886–7 S.B.A. exhibition of two Whistler portraits, both in very much the same pose: Maud as *Harmony in Black, No. 10*, and Beatrice as *Harmony in Red: Lamplight*. The following winter William Stott showed *Venus Born of the Sea Foam*, for which Maud was the nude model. It was described by one critic as depicting 'instead of a goddess . . . a red-haired Topsy'; Whistler and Stott had a much-publicized row about it. Whistler put an end to public gossip by marrying Beatrice Godwin on 11 August 1888. Their relationship, which appears to have been a successful one, lasted until Beatrice died of cancer in 1896, after which Whistler appointed her younger sister Rosalind as his ward and executrix.

Whistler's reputation in England in the late 1880s was founded as much on reports of the distinctions he received abroad as it was on the judgement of his art at home. In November 1888 he was elected an honorary member of the Royal Academy of Fine Arts in Munich, and in April the following year he was given a dinner in London to celebrate the award of a first-class medal from Munich and the Cross of St Michael of Bavaria. From both the Amsterdam International Exhibition and the Paris Universal Exhibition of 1889 he was awarded gold medals. He was made a Chevalier of the Légion d'Honneur, thanks to his promotion in Paris by Duret and Mallarmé. He travelled extensively: to Holland and Belgium with his brother William and sister-in-law, the former Helen Ionides, in the autumn of 1887, where he stopped at Ostend, Brussels and Bruges to make a series of etchings of the old town; to the Eure and Loire valleys of France on a working honeymoon, in September 1888, where he made etchings of the Renaissance architecture; and to Amsterdam the following year, where he produced some of the most refined etchings of his career.

In an interview on his return to London he described his latest work as an elaboration and combination of the two stages which had gone before, contrasting it first with the 'hard detail of the beginner' represented by the 'Thames Set', and secondly with the etchings of Venice which he called 'Impressionist'. 'Impressionism', Sickert wrote in 1889, 'probably conveys to most people the idea of a very large crop of funny frames containing very small pictures which you can't make out', meaning Whistler, who 'has always repudiated with emphasis its application to him or his work'. As understood to mean bright colours applied haphazardly, this sort of art was detested by Whistler. His technical means, taught by Gleyre and demonstrated by Whistler himself at the Académie Carmen he opened for students in Paris in 1898, consisted in the systematic arrangement of colours on the palette before any were placed on the canvas, so that the picture is 'finished when all trace of the means used to bring about the end has disappeared'. In his 'Propositions', conversation and teaching, he always emphasized that art was a 'science', and that the great art of the past, Canaletto's and Guardi's and the Dutch art of the

La Belle Dame Paresseuse, *1894,
lithograph (W.62). This is a portrait of
the artist's wife Beatrice.*

seventeenth century he admired most of all, such as Hals's, Terborch's, and Vermeer's, was the result of 'exact knowledge' of the painter's craft, and never of 'cleverness'. Observations of this sort came readily to him in his late years, when he often identified ambitions for his own art with those of artists, such as Hogarth and Velázquez, that he also revered.

By 1890, thanks mainly to French writers, Whistler's art could no longer be thought of as being 'like' either nature, or 'the coloured photograph kind of thing'. It could only be recognized for what it was, a Whistler. 'Nature is catching up,' was his reply to a remark intended to compliment him on the verisimilitude of his art. 'Why drag in Velázquez?' had been his answer in 1884 to a similar reference to the relationship of his art with that of the great Spanish master. Whistler was asking the same question he posed in another way in the 'Ten O'Clock' lecture. 'Why this lifting of the brow in deprecation of the present – this pathos in reference to the past?' Baudelaire, in criticizing the meaningless academic mythologies of the Salon, had issued a challenge which Manet, the Impressionists, and Whistler had already met in their art. Although an admirer of Manet's 'powerful handling', Whistler later came to disapprove of his *plein-air* conversion to Impressionism in the mid-1870s, condemning him for being a 'student' who followed the fashion for realism he himself had abandoned in the late 1860s.

By 1900, when he made these remarks about Manet – who had died in 1883 – Whistler had lived to see Impressionism succeeded by the post-Impressionist painting of Seurat, Gauguin and their followers, whose art implicitly invoked an acknowledgement of the continuity of the classical tradition. Whistler constantly emphasized this in his own work, especially in the pastels and lithographs of draped figures and dancers in the later

1880s and 1890s. He stood in awe of Degas's art, in which he recognized the technical mastery he coveted for himself. 'As far as painting is concerned, there is only Degas and myself,' he said, always parrying the many requests he received to take part in international exhibitions with the question 'Have you got Degas?' He was nevertheless unable to approve Degas's subject-matter, for the same reason that he disliked Manet's *Olympia*. A passionate exchange took place in Degas's studio between the two great artists, with Whistler pacing up and down, reiterating 'non, non, non, non', in front of his friend's paintings of laundresses and ballet-girls. It was the subject's lack of decorum, rather than the way it was expressed, which Whistler disapproved of. It was logical, therefore, that when Edouard Dujardin, the editor of the Symbolist *Revue Indépendante*, had asked Whistler for drawings to reproduce for the November 1886 issue – for which Mallarmé translated the 'Ten O'Clock' lecture two years later – he should choose studies of nude girls which he reworked from pastels on brown paper dating from his most 'Ingriste' period of the late 1860s or early 1870s. The lightly clad female figures, dancing girls and mother-and-child subjects he made in the late 1880s and 1890s are totally unspecific as to time and place. If their drapery and backgrounds are brilliantly modified by the addition of pastel in ultramarine blue, yellow, green or vermilion, the result is a softened neo-classicism more reminiscent of the eighteenth than of the nineteenth century. They evoke Watteau as much as Ingres.

Whistler eventually achieved his ambition of more than 20 years before, to be 'viciously French', just as the stovepipe top hat with a straight brim which Frank Harris described him wearing in the street in the 1880s shouted at the passers-by, 'I'm French, and proud of it!' The late pastels of nude female figures were Whistler's timeless response to the most mercilessly specific of Degas's uncompromising modern nudes. In Paris in the 1890s he felt more at home than he did in London. He was friendly with French artists such as Boldini, Helleu, Puvis de Chavannes, Rodin, Alfred Stevens and Aman-Jean. As well as the American and Scots artists who visited him at the Rue du Bac, he was much in demand as a guest of Montesquiou's aristocratic circle around the Comtesse de Greffulhe, the members of Proust's future cast of characters; with them, though, he told his wife, he felt uncomfortable, preferring Mallarmé and the company of those for whom art was a professional activity rather than a social one.

As the economic power of the United States increased in the closing years of the century, in part at England's expense, and the other European nations asserted their independence, so definitions of nationality in art began to alter, especially at the big international exhibitions such as those in Paris, where Whistler had first been drawn in 1855. With England now of little or no consequence as a showplace for new forms of artistic expression, in the last decade of Whistler's life the stage for his art necessarily became an international one. England, where he had lived for 30 years, had provided him with a small stage where, compared with some of his English contemporaries, he had earned a relatively small living. From the vantage point of his 56 years in 1890, he could observe the shifts of power and choose the most propitious moment to participate. The acknowledgement of eventual fame which greeted the retrospective exhibition of 43 of his paintings shown at the Goupil Gallery, London, in 1892 – on the final day there were nearly 2000 visitors – did not come from the English camp, which was still divided over his art, but was the product of the combined entrepreneurial forces of Scotland, a small but artistically emergent nation, and the initiative of American journalism.

It was not the first time Whistler had called for reinforcements from outside the mainstream European cultural arena, whether Paris, Brussels or Munich, where he exhibited regularly. He turned instead to a Celtic nation that was more appropriate to his own origins. In 1888 Whistler had tried to sell his portrait of the modern Scots philosopher Thomas Carlyle to the National Portrait Gallery in Edinburgh; its eventual purchase, by the Corporation of Glasgow in 1891, was principally due to the support given him by the group of Scottish artists known as the 'Glasgow Boys', who had exhibited first in London, and then in Munich in 1890, to international acclaim. The Scots artists organized a petition, which was presented to Glasgow Corporation. Thus from Glasgow came the first public recognition of Whistler's art in Great Britain, and the first official demand anywhere for one of his pictures.

Unlike their Edinburgh colleagues, some of whom lived in London and relied on the Royal Academy, the 'Glasgow Boys' were more in tune with developments in Paris, where many of them had trained and become familiar with European realism such as the Dutch, Barbizon and Impressionist styles of painting. They were also well acquainted with Whistler's work and his 'Ten O'Clock' philosophy, which was much respected and its precepts emulated by artists north of the border. Giving them wholehearted support abroad at this time was the American journalist and friend of Whistler, Sheridan Ford, an art correspondent in Paris. His wife, Mary Bacon Martin, represented in London and Paris one of the biggest decorating firms in New York, and was no less interested in Whistler and the Scots artists. So strong was Ford's support of Henry, Hornel, Guthrie, Walton, Melville and other Glasgow artists that continental readers were more familiar with such names and their achievements than Glasgow was itself. Ford's support of such an eccentric 'Celtic fringe' in his Salon reviews annoyed the French 'glue-pots' in Paris, and so, of course, delighted Whistler, whom Ford also fulsomely publicized in his regular columns in the London edition of the *New York Herald*.

When Ford had the inspired idea of compiling Whistler's printed letters, *bons mots*, epithets, and other literary ephemera for an amusing and popular book under the title *The Gentle Art of Making Enemies*, Whistler readily agreed. The rest is bibliographic history. Whistler soon came to realize what a golden egg could be his, and pursued Ford through the Belgian and American courts to have his book suppressed. Whistler's own version, much enlarged and designed by him down to every typographic detail and manic butterfly, was published in brown and yellow hard covers by William Heinemann (who became a close friend) in June 1890, and dedicated to 'The rare Few, who, early in Life, had rid themselves of the Friendship of the Many'. It soon ran to several editions.

Before the portrait of Carlyle was sent to Glasgow early in 1891, the director of the Goupil Gallery in London, David Croal Thomson, also a Scotsman, agreed to show it in a room to itself in his Bond Street gallery. Thomson then arranged for Whistler the sale in 1891 of *Arrangement in Grey and Black: Portrait of the Artist's Mother* to the French government through M. Joyant of the Goupil's branch in Paris, where, thanks to the efforts of Duret and Mallarmé, it was hung in the Musée du Luxembourg. As a follow-up to these efforts on Whistler's behalf, Thomson gave over the Goupil Gallery to the large exhibition of his paintings which Whistler organized in March 1892, together with the publication of a catalogue, again containing previous reviews and criticism; this sold in its thousands. Although no sales from the exhibition were transacted, within a year of its closing Thomson had

managed to transfer from their first owners more than half of the pictures in the show, at prices double and three times the sums originally paid for them. As a result of the mutual trust between Whistler, Thomson, and the Glasgow dealer Alexander Reid, to whom Whistler consigned several of his important pictures, the price of Whistler's art rose steadily. Thereafter he was more or less able to select the buyers of his work, and prevent it remaining in England if he chose to.

When in 1898 Whistler founded in London, with John Lavery as his vice-president, the International Society of Sculptors, Painters and Gravers, his specific aim was the 'non-recognition' of nationality in art which he had pursued in relation to his own exhibiting career. The medals and honours awarded for different categories of art, divided by nationality, were eschewed by the International Society, the intention of which, Whistler explained, was to 'break through the wearisome routine of the annual shows', because 'the British public is kept completely in the dark as to the real nature of the Art movement throughout the world'. The first exhibition, held at Prince's Skating Rink, Knightsbridge, contained 42 French, 20 German, 16 American, 41 Scottish, and 104 English artists, as well as artists from Austria, Holland, Italy, Switzerland and Scandinavia. Although the English artists included some whom Whistler described as 'typical mediocrities – and . . . little groups of lunchers at the Arts Club', the exhibition was representative of all recent developments in world art, from Impressionism to Symbolism and *art nouveau*. Among the artists were Bonnard, Denis, Cézanne, Lautrec, Klimt, Rodin, Thoma, Toorop, Böcklin, Beardsley, Puvis de Chavannes, Segantini, Manet and Degas, as well as a heavy contingent from Scotland, and many now less well-known contributors to international modernism at the turn of the century. The exhibition was hung by

Whistler, regardless of nationality or school, to suggest that modern painting originated with Manet, Degas and himself; and with the intention of marginalizing the Impressionism practised by the New English Art Club, which Whistler considered only 'a raft', in contrast with the 'battleship' of the International.

Whistler's last years were lived in the shadow of his wife's final illness, which for nearly two years he preferred not to face, but almost certainly knew would prove fatal. The young American artist Edmund Wuerpel remembers him in Paris at this time, when 'he would quite frequently lose himself on the boulevards and in cafés of the city, remaining away from home for hours and causing much uneasiness there'. After Beatrice's death in 1896 he wandered restlessly from one hotel to another in Paris and London, staying for long periods with the publisher William Heinemann, but travelling almost as much as he had in previous years: to France, Holland, Italy, and in 1900 to Marseilles and Corsica to recover his failing health. His affairs were looked after by his sister-in-law, Rosalind Birnie Philip, who acted as secretary, and with whose family he lived at 72 Cheyne Walk for the final year of his life. Arthur Symons remembered meeting him at a dinner party in 1900:

> I never saw any one so feverishly alive as this little, old man, with his bright, withered cheeks, over which the skin was drawn tightly, his darting eyes, under their prickly bushes of eyebrow, his fantastically creased black and white curls of hair, his bitter and subtle mouth, and, above all, his exquisite hands, never at rest . . . In what he said of his own work and of others, there was neither vanity nor humility; he knew quite well what in his art he had

The Siesta, *1896, lithograph (W.122). Done at the Savoy Hotel, this shows Whistler's wife Beatrice shortly before her death from cancer.*

mastered and what others had failed to master. But it was chiefly of art in the abstract that he talked, and of the artist's attitude towards nature and towards his materials. He only said to me, I suppose, what he had been saying and writing for fifty years; it was his gospel, which he had preached mockingly, that he might disconcert the mockers; but he said it all like one possessed of a conviction, and as if he were stating that conviction with his first ardour . . . No man made more enemies, or deserved better friends. He never cared, or was able, to distinguish between them. They changed places at an opinion or for an idea.

In spite of his personal loss, his last years were no less notable for the campaigns he prosecuted on behalf of his own art and that of other artists. He supported Joseph Pennell, whose lithographs Sickert claimed were not original works of art because they were drawn on transfer paper, a process Whistler regularly used himself, and which he testified to in the successful lawsuit Pennell brought in 1897. In 1895 he defended an action brought by Sir William Eden, whose wife's portrait he had painted and then withheld, because of the unsatisfactory manner in which he considered Eden had attempted to pay for it. Although Whistler was first ordered to hand over the work, and to pay Eden damages, on appeal he was granted the right to retain it. In so doing he established an important precedent in French law, which had previously been understood only informally, namely that the artist must be free to withhold a work with which he is dissatisfied, until such time as it pleases him to submit it, while accepting the liability to restore fees paid in advance and to make good his patron's expenses. Whistler published his account of the protracted proceedings in *Eden versus Whistler: The Baronet and the Butterfly* in 1899. In 1898 an atelier in Paris was opened by Carmen Rossi, one of Whistler's models. With the American sculptor Frederick MacMonnies he became, for a brief time, its visitor, imparting to students of all nationalities, particularly Americans, his scientific methods of colour harmony, achieved by disciplined preparation of the palette, and illustrated by his 'Propositions', which were translated into French by Duret to hang on the walls of the studio.

As his life drew to its close, Whistler was beset at every turn by writers, some competent, others much less so, who were anxious to write about him and his art. In order to prevent the worst he consented, in 1900, to allow his fellow Americans, Elizabeth Robins Pennell, a talented art critic, and her husband Joseph, an etcher and illustrator much influenced by Whistler, to write a two-volume biography that would be published by William Heinemann. Joseph first met Whistler in 1884. Thereafter the couple shadowed him, making sporadic notes, until they began a systematic Journal in 1900, in which they diligently recorded much of what they heard from Whistler of his past life: of his reverence for the military ethos of West Point; of his views on the present, especially where they concerned English art, and on the unsuccessful progress of the British army in its campaign against the Boers in South Africa. While their biography, eventually published in 1908, and the Journal on which they based it, published in 1921, remain invaluable, their judgement was less than dispassionate, since they de-

Firelight No. 2 – Joseph Pennell, *1896, lithograph (W.105)*.

ferred to their subject's every whim and prejudice, and set down all that Whistler said with a critical insouciance amounting to naivety. They ultimately rendered Whistler a disservice in the eyes of posterity, not just in reiterating his anglophobia, but by emphasizing his American nationality. Since Whistler never produced art which could narrowly be described as being 'American', the Pennells' insistence on his nationality contributed little to an understanding of it. Furthermore, the exaggerated claims they made for the superiority of his art over that of his contemporaries, and their disgust at twentieth-century modernism, the manifestations of which occurred more in France and Germany than in the United States in the years before the First World War, effectively denied Whistler a place in the continuity of modernist expression in Europe, which a more objective and considered account might have encouraged.

Whistler's contribution to art was as much the result of what he did, said or wrote about it, as by what he made. The influence of his ideas on the public and critical perception of art, and on the role of the artist in society, was immense and far-reaching, both as the cause of a reaction and as a source of emulation. 'Whistler may stand', wrote Frank Harris, 'as a type of the great artist for many a year to come.' His professional career illustrates, for the first time, the modernist paradox of the Western artist, in the age of mechanical reproduction, who simultaneously requires to live by society, but by the art he produces necessarily has to rise above it. While such a dilemma was the result of post-industrial capitalism, and artists in the twentieth century now work within its constraints, the richly inventive way in which Whistler conducted his life, and created art, provides multiple examples of how this dilemma might still be resolved.

THE PLATES

Portrait of Whistler with Hat, 1858

46.3 × 38.1 cm. Freer Gallery of Art, Washington DC

This self-portrait was probably painted in the Rue Campagne-Première, Paris, where Whistler was living in June 1858. It was given by Whistler to his friend, the French artist Ernest Delannoy, Whistler's companion on the walking tour he made of eastern France, Luxembourg and the Rhineland in 1858, which resulted in the *Twelve Etchings after Nature*, or the 'French Set' as it became known. Théodore Duret found in it the influence of Rembrandt's *Head of a Young Man* in the Louvre. Although it is probable that Whistler had not met Courbet when he painted it, the frank realism and broad brush-strokes, as well as the bold signature in red, all evoke his art and are consistent with an attempt to emulate seventeenth-century Dutch painting, particularly Rembrandt's, which was much admired among modern realist artists in France in the late 1850s.

Butcher's Shop, Saverne, 1858

21.7 × 14.4 cm. Freer Gallery of Art, Washington DC

This early watercolour dates from Whistler's walking and etching tour of eastern France in the summer of 1858. Saverne is a village to the north-east of Nancy. There he etched *Street at Saverne* (p. 12), its dramatic *chiaroscuro* being reminiscent of the work of the French etcher Charles Méryon. But instead of the etching's plunging perspective, Whistler painted the butcher's shop almost head-on, as he did the shop-fronts he regularly etched and painted in the 1880s and 1890s (see pp. 111, 121).

Boutique du Boucher
Saverne

Harmony in Green and Rose: The Music Room, 1860/61

95.5 × 70.8 cm. Freer Gallery of Art, Washington DC

The subject of 'The Morning Call', as *Harmony in Green and Rose* was first called, is set in the music room at 62 Sloane Street, the home of Whistler's half-sister Deborah and her husband Francis Seymour Haden. It shows Deborah's image, reflected in the mirror to the left, her daughter Annie, and, standing in riding dress, Isabella Boott, a niece of Kirk Boott, the founder of Lowell, Massachusetts, who had first invited Whistler's father to Lowell in 1834. Isabella's eldest sister had married Haden's younger brother; the picture is thus emblematic of Whistler's family ties between America and Britain. Significantly, it was given by Whistler's mother to her daughter-in-law, Julia, the wife of Whistler's half-brother George, after which Whistler did not see it again until it was exhibited at the Goupil Gallery in 1892. He then described it, in a letter to his wife, as 'quite primitive – but such *sunshine*! none of the Dutchmen to *compare* with it – and such colour!' By 'Dutchmen' he may have had in mind such seventeenth-century artists as Terborch and De Hooch, who were much admired by Whistler, Fantin and Degas. *Harmony in Green and Rose* was the second picture Whistler painted in the music room of 62 Sloane Street. The first, *At the Piano* (Taft Museum, Cincinnati), was shown, to some acclaim, at the Royal Academy exhibition of 1860, after being rejected by the Paris Salon in 1859. *Harmony in Green and Rose* was obviously intended as a follow-up to the success of *At the Piano*, although Whistler did not carry out the intention he had in 1864 of sending it to the Salon. Its more sophisticated spatial complexity may also reflect the influence of Japanese prints.

Blue and Silver: Blue Wave, Biarritz, 1862

61 × 87.6 cm. Hill-Stead Museum, Farmington, Connecticut

Whistler travelled to the Basses-Pyrénées in October 1862, with the express intention of painting seascapes. He stayed in Guéthary, four miles to the south of Biarritz. He appears to have been commissioned by an unknown client to paint a marine subject on a fairly large scale, with fishermen and women (including a portrait of Jo), a sailor in a red shirt, rocks, and a rough sea breaking in the foreground. The subject sounds a fairly conventional one, similar to pictures by English artists such as Clarkson Stanfield, or possibly James Clarke Hook, whom Whistler admired, and whose successful marine paintings resulted in his election to the Royal Academy in 1860. In a letter to Fantin from Guéthary, Whistler described the breakers as being 'superb . . . so solid that they seem to be cut from black stone – and then on the surface in the middle great waves smash themselves against two separate rocks that you can see *in* the sea'. This description resembles *The Blue Wave*. It is probable that, in abandoning the marine with figures, which he complained to Fantin he was unable to complete because of the weather, he was left with this. Thirty years did not dim Whistler's memory of the experience which he had put on canvas in 1862. In 1892 he wrote to his wife, describing this painting in the Goupil Gallery exhibition: 'You never saw such a sea – absolutely *sculptured* out of the most brilliant blue and green and violet!'

Wapping, 1861–4

71.1 × 101.6 cm. National Gallery of Art, Washington DC

Wapping was probably begun in 1861 in Rotherhithe, where Whistler was then making the 'Thames Set' etchings. Whistler intended that the subject should evoke his etchings, and show a complex verbal exchange between three figures seated on the balcony of an inn on the south side of the river opposite the Wapping shore. He explained in a letter to Fantin that he had given the girl (for whom his mistress Joanna Hiffernan sat) 'a real expression', as if she was saying to the man on the far right, a sailor, '"That's all very well, old boy, but I've seen others", you know she's winking and making fun of him.' X-rays of the picture show that the 'old man' in the centre, first painted wearing a white shirt, was originally much closer to the girl, suggesting that Whistler meant to convey an element of tension between the girl and her two admirers. Perhaps he was even suggesting she was a prostitute in league with a 'protector' as she 'set up' a client, a situation Whistler could easily have witnessed at first hand in the low-life dives off the Ratcliffe Highway. Clearly the scheme proved too ambitious for him; he probably laid the canvas off in 1861 until late in 1863 or early 1864, when Alphonse Legros posed for the central figure as 'a sort of Spanish sailor', and the narrative element was much reduced. All along Whistler had intended to show *Wapping* in Paris, and warned Fantin not to tell Courbet about it. His original conception not only proved too difficult to realize, but was altogether too *risqué* a subject for a public exhibition. In toning it down he made it suitable for the Royal Academy, where it was shown in 1864. Although it was praised as a vigorous portrait of river-life, the 'ugly' figures did not meet with critical approval.

Grey and Silver: Old Battersea Reach, 1863

49.5 × 67.9 cm. The Art Institute of Chicago

This painting, called simply 'Battersea' when it was exhibited at the Royal Academy in 1867, was one of Whistler's first Thames pictures, painted soon after he moved to 7 Lindsey Row, Chelsea, in March 1863. The viewpoint, just upstream of Battersea Bridge (out of the picture to the left), is taken from outside Whistler's house, and shows the Battersea shore with the graphite-burning chimneys of Morgan's Patent Plumbago Crucible Company's Works, then the world's largest makers of crucibles, and the spire of St Mary's Church, Battersea, to the right. In the distance, faintly glimpsed closing off the horizon, can be seen Battersea Railway Bridge, which had only just been opened in 1863. The barges in the middle are coal-heavers, preparing to off-load their cargoes at Johnson's coal wharf which was downstream of Battersea Bridge; the boats in the foreground probably belonged to Greaves's boatyard, located on the Lindsey Row waterfront. The Greaves family, particularly Walter and Henry, became familiar with Whistler, rowed him on the river, and were his assistants and pupils. This part of the Thames had been a popular subject with English artists, who concentrated on what was once an essentially rural scene before the building of the Chelsea Embankment (after which much of the river trade shown in Whistler's picture was re-located). Whistler chooses instead to emphasize the changing landscape, the industrial life and the commercial activity of the river, just as he had done with the 'Thames Set' etchings he made downstream between 1859 and 1861.

Symphony in White, No. 1: The White Girl, 1862

214.6 × 108 cm. National Gallery of Art, Washington DC

When it was shown as 'The Woman in White' in a mixed exhibition in Berners Street, after being rejected by the Royal Academy in 1862, the critic of the *Athenaeum* complained that it did not resemble the heroine of Wilkie Collins's novel of the same name, which was then enjoying colossal public acclaim. Whistler replied, in his first letter to the press, that his only intention had been to 'represent a girl dressed in white standing in front of a white curtain'. While Whistler's claim never to have read the novel may be true, he could not have been unaware of the fashion for white – dresses, accessories, even waltzes and quadrilles named after the book – which Collins's popular success precipitated. When shown at the Salon des Refusés in 1863, it shared with Manet's *Déjeuner sur l'herbe* (Paris, Musée d'Orsay) a similar *succès d'éxécration*, which Zola described in his novel *L'Oeuvre* of 1886. Both works were notable for their evasion of an explicit narrative; both avoided any specific commitment to the sexual content of their subjects. In Whistler's case critics either discussed the picture in terms of how it was painted, or else attempted to find a meaning for it, but generally found one approach incompatible with the other. For Théophile Thoré, the girl's expression and her dishevelled appearance (for which Joanna Hiffernan was again the model) suggested precedents in English art. Paul Mantz called the picture a 'Symphony in White', and justified it by association with the practice of eighteenth-century French artists, such as Jean-Baptiste Oudry, who painted 'white on white'. But the critic Jules Castagnary, a friend of Courbet's, explained it by supplying an appropriately realist scenario, which represented the girl on her honeymoon, a legitimized version of Greuze's symbolic portrait in the Louvre, *La Cruche Cassée*, a young girl carrying a broken pitcher. Retrospectively, Whistler chose to emphasize the picture's abstract qualities by retitling it *Symphony in White, No. 1*, after painting *The Little White Girl* (p. 61) and *Symphony in White, No. 3* (p. 69).

Caprice in Purple and Gold, No. 2: The Golden Screen, 1864

50.2 × 68.7 cm. Freer Gallery of Art, Washington DC

Whistler's exotic *Japonaiserie* evokes, in oriental translation, John Everett Millais's double portrait of two young girls sitting in front of a folding screen, *Leisure Hours*, which was shown in the Royal Academy exhibition of 1864. Whistler's picture, exhibited the following year as *The Golden Screen*, shows his Irish mistress and model for *The White Girl* and *The Little White Girl* (pp. 57, 61), Joanna Hiffernan, draped in a Japanese kimono. Behind her is a Japanese screen, probably of the Tosa school; woodblock prints by Hiroshige are strewn around; and an oriental lacquered box is in the left foreground. Some of these items were probably obtained by Whistler at Madame de Soye's *La Porte chinoise*, a Paris shop which specialized in fashionable *Japonisme*, and where Whistler is known to have been a customer in the 1860s. The contents of the picture provide important evidence for the Japanese art owned by Whistler, and suggest the nature of its influence on his own painting at this time. Like other artists, such as the etcher Bracquemond in Paris, who soon after the opening up of Japan to the West in 1853 was influenced by the flat space of Hokusai's woodblock prints, Whistler, in some of his 'Thames Set' etchings, adopted similar compositional devices of an un-occidental nature. In *The Golden Screen* he combines these – by tilting the foreground plane and denying the perspective illusionism associated with Western art – with the brilliant colour of Japanese prints such as Hiroshige's, which he treats with the same colourful intensity as he does the rest of the picture.

Symphony in White, No. 2: The Little White Girl, 1864

76 × 51 cm. Tate Gallery, London

The mood of *The Little White Girl*, as it was called when shown at the Royal Academy exhibition of 1864, and for which Joanna Hiffernan again posed, evokes that of the images Dante Gabriel Rossetti was painting at this time, such as his *Beata Beatrix* (Tate Gallery). Whistler had met Rossetti two years before, and the *Little White Girl* dates from the height of their friendship. At this time he also had a close friendship with Swinburne, whose verses 'Before the Mirror' were attached to the frame for the picture's first exhibition, and printed in the Academy catalogue. In a letter to Whistler Swinburne wrote that Rossetti had praised his verse 'highly, and I think myself the idea is pretty: I know it was entirely and only suggested to me by the picture . . . ' In 1902, after his quarrel with Swinburne, Whistler wrote that the poem was 'a rare and graceful tribute from the poet to the painter – a noble recognition of work by the production of a nobler one'. Whereas Rossetti had previously endowed subjects derived from literature with his own imagination, here Whistler demonstrates that a modern subject in painting can be translated back into verse. It marks the coequal status between painter and poet which Whistler shared with Swinburne in the 1860s. In his review of the 1864 Academy, Rossetti's brother, the critic William Michael Rossetti, drew attention to its relationship with *The White Girl* (p. 57), and favourably compared its 'delicate harmony' with the 'daring force' of *Esther*, a work by John Everett Millais in the same exhibition.

Sea and Rain, 1865

50.8 × 72.7 cm. University of Michigan Museum of Art

On 20 October 1865 Whistler was in Trouville, with Joanna Hiffernan, and wrote to his friend Luke Ionides: 'I am staying here to finish 2 or 3 seapieces which I wish to bring back with me. I believe they will be fine – and worth quite anything of the kind I have ever done. This is a charming place – although now the season is quite over and everyone has left – but the effects of sea and sky are finer than during the milder weather.' In Trouville Whistler painted half a dozen seascapes of this kind, all of which, as his letter indicates, were intended to emphasize different weather conditions at different times of the day, from morning to evening. *Sea and Rain* was the largest, and Whistler chose it to send to the Royal Academy exhibition of 1867. Also at Trouville at this time was Courbet, whom Whistler depicted in the foreground of *Harmony in Blue and Silver: Trouville* (Isabella Stewart Gardner Museum, Boston) gazing out to sea. In his turn Courbet painted Jo as *La Belle Irlandaise* (Metropolitan Museum of Art, New York), emphasizing her luxuriant Pre-Raphaelite hair in homage to her portrait as *The White Girl* (p. 57). While the seascapes Whistler painted at Trouville are often compared with Courbet's, they bear a much greater resemblance to those by Manet of 1864.

Rose and Silver: The Princess from the Land of Porcelain, 1863–4

199.9 × 116.1 cm. Freer Gallery of Art, Washington DC

The model for *The Princess from the Land of Porcelain* was Christine Spartali, a girl whose beauty was much admired in the Rossetti-Swinburne circle of the mid-1860s. Whistler obviously hoped that it would be bought by her father Michael Spartali, a rich Greek merchant, later the Greek Consul-General in London, but significantly he objected to it 'as a portrait'. Whistler then sent it to the Paris Salon of 1865, where its overt *Japonisme* and brilliant colour met with hostility as well as praise. In the same exhibition Fantin-Latour showed *Le Toast*, which included portraits of Manet and Whistler. Although it was intended, like the *Homage to Delacroix* of the year before, as a naturalist manifesto, critics such as Paul Mantz sensed that both Whistler, 'the painter of fantasies', and Manet, 'a visionary', had already exceeded the realist canon they had previously embraced in their art.

The Princess was bought by Frederick Leyland, and by November 1872 was hanging above the fireplace of his dining room at 49 Princes Gate, London. Leyland had the dining room remodelled by the architect Thomas Jeckyll, with shelves in an elaborate Anglo-Japanese style to hold his collection of blue and white porcelain, and the walls backed with old Spanish leather. Whistler thought the colour of the flowers decorating the leather, and the border of the carpet, clashed with his painting. He took it on himself to exceed Leyland's permission to modify the colour of the walls, and by September 1876 had commenced an elaborate 'Harmony in Blue and Gold' on walls and ceiling, based on the tail and breast feathers of the peacock, and including two full-sized peacocks painted on the inside of the window shutters. Leyland's refusal to pay Whistler £2,000 for the work ended their relationship, and precipitated Whistler's bankruptcy. After Leyland's death, both *The Princess* and the Peacock Room itself were acquired by the American collector Charles Lang Freer, and can now be seen reassembled in the Freer Gallery in Washington.

Symphony in Grey and Green: The Ocean, 1866–72

80.7 × 101.9 cm. Frick Collection, New York

At the end of January 1866 Whistler made a will in favour of Joanna Hiffernan and travelled to Valparaiso, where the Chileans were engaged in a war of liberation with Spain. He returned in September the same year, after avoiding any military involvement. Several reasons, none of them entirely satisfactory, have been advanced for Whistler making the journey. These include guilt at his failure to participate in the American Civil War, in which his brother William distinguished himself; the burden of Jo, who may have borne him a child; and identification with the outlawed Fenian movement, which required his hurried departure from England. Whistler painted six works during this period: three of Valparaiso, and three of the ocean on either the outward or return journey, of which *Symphony in Grey and Green: The Ocean* is one. It was first shown at the Dudley Gallery in 1872, with a decorated frame painted blue on gold, together with the first 'Nocturnes' of the Thames he exhibited under that title. As in the nocturnes, the butterfly signature in a cartouche and the asymmetric design of *Symphony in Grey and Green* reflect the influence of Japanese art. Whistler's depiction of the ocean in 1866 also bears a marked compositional resemblance to the series painted by Manet of the naval battle, an episode in the American Civil War, fought off the Cherbourg coast in 1864 between the 'Kearsage' and the 'Alabama'.

Symphony in White, No. 3, 1865–7

52 × 76.5 cm. The Barber Institute of Fine Arts, The University of Birmingham

According to W.M. Rossetti originally called 'The Two Little White Girls', this was the first work to be exhibited by Whistler with a musical title. With it Whistler clearly intended to make an important statement, for as early as August 1865 he described and sketched it in a letter to Fantin-Latour, emphasizing the line and colour of the composition. He was particularly pleased with the relationship of the arms of the two women to each other, and to the back of the sofa. Even before it was exhibited he sent it to Paris, in April 1867, to be seen by his artist friends, including Degas, who drew it in his notebook. Fantin reported to Whistler that he found it original (as did the artists Alfred Stevens and Tissot), but criticized it for being too nebulous, too much 'like a dream'. He accounted for this by the difference in their respective artistic personalities, which would soon be exacerbated as Whistler became more abstract in his painting, and his work grew apart from Fantin's. When it was shown at the Royal Academy in 1867 critics compared it with the work of the English painter Albert Moore, whom Whistler had known for about two years, and whose neo-classical figure painting and flat decorative style affected him strongly. Moore introduced Whistler to a more rigorous study of line and form, based on classical precedents such as the Elgin marbles in the British Museum, at a time when Whistler had begun to question the influence of Courbet's realism. In the year that Whistler exhibited *Symphony in White, No. 3* he explicitly repudiated Courbet, and stated to Fantin that he wished he had been a pupil of Ingres. *Symphony in White, No. 3* elicited Whistler's celebrated response to the English critic Philip Gilbert Hamerton, who complained that it was 'not precisely a symphony in white' since yellow, brown, blue, red and green also appeared. 'Does he then', wrote Whistler, 'believe that a symphony in F contains no other note, but shall be a continued repetition of F, F, F . . . ? Fool!'

The White Symphony: Three Girls, 1868

46.4 × 61.6 cm. Freer Gallery of Art, Washington DC

The 'Three Girls' composition formed one of a series of six oil sketches that William Michael Rossetti described in 1868: Whistler was 'doing on a largish scale for Leyland the subject of women with flowers, and has made coloured sketches of four or five other subjects of the like class, very promising in point of conception of colour-arrangement'. After a visit to Whistler's studio in the spring of 1868 Swinburne wrote, 'in one, a sketch for the great picture, the soft brilliant floor-work and wall-work of a garden balcony serve . . . to set forth the flowers and figures of flowerlike women'. Leyland commissioned an enlargement of the 'Three Girls' composition, and Whistler worked intermittently on it for more than ten years. Only a fragment from an enlargement, and an insubstantial copy made in 1879, which is now in the Tate Gallery, survive. Whistler intended the picture to hang in the Peacock Room, on the end wall opposite *The Princess from the Land of Porcelain* (p. 65). The arrangement of the 'Three Girls' parallels Albert Moore's *Pomegranates* (Guildhall Art Gallery, London) of 1866, and also the figures in certain Japanese prints. Whistler's intention of evoking a *Gesamtkunstwerk* with the composition is suggested by the remark he made to the American artist Otto Bacher. 'His most ambitious desire was to paint a grand concerto-like picture with the title "Full Palette" – "Just as in music", he explained, "When they employ all the instruments they make it 'Full Band'. If I can find the right kind of thing I will produce a harmony in colour corresponding to Beethoven's harmonies in sound".'

Variations in Flesh Colour and Green: The Balcony, 1864–70

61.4 × 48.8 cm. Freer Gallery of Art, Washington DC

In February 1864 Whistler was described by his mother as working on 'a group in Oriental costume on a balcony, a tea equipage of the old china'. The idea for the subject may have been suggested to him by Fantin-Latour, who was planning to paint oriental fantasies in 1863. Whereas Fantin's figures were firmly based on Western precedents, such as Veronese, Whistler's retained a strong Japanese flavour, which was emphasized throughout by the costumes, the decorative flowers, brilliant colour and asymmetric arrangement of the composition.

By 1865 Whistler had completed a version of the *Balcony* which he signed and dated. This early state, known only from a photograph, differs from the final version in the arrangement of the figures, in its lack of blossoms, and the presence of Whistler's signature and date, replaced by a butterfly in the finished picture, which was finally exhibited at the Royal Academy in 1870. In 1867 Whistler told Fantin that he intended to make a life-size version for exhibition at the Salon; a squared-up painted sketch now in the Hunterian Art Gallery of Glasgow University may relate to this unrealized ambition. Japanese prints by Harunobu and by Kiyonaga, the latter owned by Whistler, have been cited as influences. In 1870 the *Art Journal* thought it 'singular and eccentric. The picture might have been painted in Japan. It affects to be Japanese in colour, composition, and handling.' When it was shown at Durand-Ruel's gallery in Paris, early in 1873, it got an equally negative critical response. The unique combination of industrial Battersea shore with Japanese figures, in which each implicitly questions the verisimilitude of the other, was further developed with the nocturnes of the 1870s.

Variations in Pink and Grey: Chelsea, 1871/2

62.7 × 40.5 cm. Freer Gallery of Art, Washington DC

This painting shows Battersea Reach and the Chelsea waterfront to the right near Whistler's house in Lindsey Row. The interrupted wall and hoarding suggest that it was painted during the construction of the Chelsea Embankment between Chelsea Hospital and Battersea Bridge. It had been hoped that the Embankment might make London more like Baron Haussmann's Paris. *The Building News* suggested that it might be 'converted into a boulevard . . . lined with cafés, restaurants, little paradises and pavilions, with marble tables, coffee stalls, and pretty paraphernalia of the kind'. The elegantly dressed ladies in Whistler's picture, some with parasols, as in Japanese prints, seem to be promenading in anticipation of these modern pleasures, which never in fact materialized.

Harmony in Grey and Green: Miss Cicely Alexander, 1872–3

190 × 98 cm. Tate Gallery, London

Cicely Alexander was the second daughter of the London banker and art collector W.C. Alexander. Her father was the first to buy a nocturne, and he commissioned Whistler to paint portraits of his two daughters, both of which are now in the Tate Gallery. Whistler designed the dress for the portrait, and advised the sitter's mother to obtain fine Indian muslin, either from a second-hand shop near Leicester Square, or from Farmer and Roger in Regent Street. 'In case the Indian muslin is not to be had', he wrote, 'then the usual fine muslin of which ladies' evening dresses are made up will do – the blue well taken out – and the little dress afterwards done up by the laundress with a little starch to make the frills and skirts etc stand out – of course not an atom of blue!' During Whistler's lifetime, *Harmony in Grey and Green: Miss Cicely Alexander* was one of his most widely travelled pictures. Between 1884, when it was exhibited at the Paris Salon, and 1899, when it was shown at the Venice Biennale, it was also seen in Brussels, Munich, London (five times), and Dublin. After the *Mother*, it became one of Whistler's best-known works, and is arguably one of the great portraits of the nineteenth century. Of all his works it was the one most often compared to Velázquez. Huysmans wrote that 'its broad finish makes it appear barely painted, and it lives an intense life of its own, just like a Velázquez, painted boldly with such beautiful impasto in a range of silver greys . . . quite apart from physical appearance, there is also a supernatural side to this mysterious, slightly ghostly painter, which to some degree justifies the word "spiritualist" used by Desnoyers' (who had written about *The White Girl* in these terms in 1863). For George Moore, it was 'the most beautiful in the world. I know very well that it has not the profound magic of the Infantes of Velázquez in the Louvre; but for pure magic of inspiration, is it not more delightful? . . . There is also something of Velázquez in the black notes of the shoes. Those blacks – are they not perfectly observed? How light and dry the colour is! How heavy and shiny it would have become in other hands! Notice, too, that in the frock nowhere is there a single touch of pure white, and yet it is all white – a rich, luminous white that makes every other white in the gallery seem either chalky or dirty . . . The eye travels over the canvas seeking a fault. In vain; nothing has been omitted that might have been included, nothing has been included that might have been omitted. There is much in Velázquez that is stronger, but nothing in his world ever seemed to me so perfect as this picture.'

Nocturne in Blue and Silver, 1871/2

44.4 × 60.3 cm. Fogg Art Museum, Cambridge, MA

This is one of Whistler's first nocturnes. It was shown in the Grosvenor Gallery exhibition of 1877, and was presented in court as evidence in the trial for libel which Whistler brought against Ruskin in November 1878. It shows the Battersea shore from Lindsey Row, with the chimneys of Morgan's Crucible Works and the spire of St Mary's Church, Battersea, to the right. At the Ruskin trial Whistler was asked by his counsel to tell the court the meaning of the word 'nocturne'. 'I have, perhaps', said Whistler, 'meant rather to indicate an artistic interest alone in the work, divesting the picture of any anecdotal interest which might have been otherwise attached to it . . . Among my works are some night pieces; and I have chosen the word nocturne because it generalizes and simplifies the whole set of them. It is an accident that I have happened upon the terms that are used in music, and very often have I been misunderstood from that fact, it having been supposed that I intended some way or other to show a connection between the two arts, whereas I had no such intention.' It was Leyland, an amateur interpreter of Chopin, who had first suggested the name 'nocturne' for what Whistler had previously called his 'moonlights'. The *Nocturne in Blue and Silver*, presented by Whistler to Mrs Leyland in 1872, commemorates her husband's contribution to Whistler's art at this time.

Arrangement in Grey and Black:
Portrait of the Artist's Mother, 1871

144.3 × 165.2 cm. Musée du Louvre, Paris

Whistler's mother, Anna Matilda McNeill, first posed standing for two or three days, but when this proved too tiring, she adopted a sitting position. Whistler took three months to complete this portrait, over the summer of 1871. It was shown in the Royal Academy exhibition of 1872, allegedly only after Sir William Boxall – who had exhibited his portrait of Whistler there in 1849 – threatened to resign if it were not accepted. It was Whistler's last submission to the Academy. In November 1891 the portrait was bought for the Musée du Luxembourg for 4000 francs, largely through the intervention of Duret, Mallarmé, and Roger Marx. In a letter to her sister, Kate Palmer, the sitter described Whistler's progress with the work. 'Jemie had no nervous fears in painting his Mothers portrait for it was to please himself and not to be paid for in other coin, only at one or two difficult points when I heard him ejaculate "No! I can't get it right! it is impossible to do as it ought to be done perfectly!" I silently lifted my heart, that it might be as the Net cast down in the Lake at the Lords will, as I observed his trying again, and oh my grateful rejoicing in spirit as suddenly my dear Son would exclaim, "Oh Mother it is mastered, it is beautiful!" and he would kiss me for it!' In spite of Whistler's imprecation – 'what can or ought the public to care about the identity of the portrait?' – from the start his powerful intellectual grasp of the Protestant character did not go unnoticed. Emilia Pattison, in a review of the 1872 Academy, thought it 'brings up a vision of the typical Huguenot interior – protestantism in a Catholic country'. George Moore, writing of Whistler in 1892, believed that in the portrait he 'told the story of his soul more fully than elsewhere. That soul, strangely alive to all that is delicate and illusive in Nature, found perhaps its fullest expression in that grave old Puritan lady looking through the quiet refinement of her grey room, sitting in solemn profile in all the quiet habit of her long life'.

For all Whistler's efforts to emphasize the formal qualities of her portrait, after Swinburne in 1888 had castigated him for denying its 'intense pathos of significance and tender depth of expression', Whistler's most famous work became a universal symbol of motherhood, culminating in its representation on a stamp to commemorate Mother's Day in America in 1934.

Nocturne: Blue and Gold – Old Battersea Bridge, 1872–3

66.6 × 50.2 cm. Tate Gallery, London

The most Japanese of all Whistler's nocturnes, this painting contains elements from several of Hiroshige's prints, specifically from the series *One Hundred Views of Edo* and *Fifty-three Views of the Tokaido*. Given that, it still shows recognizable London topography: the illuminated clock tower of Chelsea Church, and, through an arch of the bridge, a glimpse of Albert Bridge, which was first opened to traffic in August 1873. In 1877 Whistler sold it to William Graham for £100, in place of a figure picture, *Annabel Lee*, that he was unable to complete. After exhibition at the Grosvenor Gallery it was produced in court on 25 November 1878 as evidence in Whistler's suit against Ruskin; the following exchange took place:

Attorney-General: 'What was the subject of the nocturne in blue and silver [*sic*] belonging to Mr Graham?'

Whistler: 'That . . . represents Battersea Bridge by moonlight.'

AG: 'Do you say that this is a correct representation of Battersea Bridge?'

W: 'I did not intend it to be a correct portrait of the bridge, but only a painting of a moonlight scene.'

Baron Huddleston: 'Is this part of the picture at the top Old Battersea Bridge?' (laughter) 'I must earnestly rebuke those who laughed.'

W: 'The pier in the centre of the picture may not be like the piers of Battersea Bridge. It was not my intention simply to make a copy of Battersea Bridge . . .'

AG: 'The prevailing colour is blue?'

W: 'Yes.'

AG: 'Are those figures on the top of the bridge intended for people?'

W: 'They are just what you like. As to what the picture represents, that depends upon who looks at it. To some persons it may represent all that I intended; to others it may represent nothing.'

AG: 'That is a barge beneath?'

W: 'Yes. I am very much flattered at your seeing that.'

AG: 'What is that mark on the right of the picture, like a cascade – is it a firework?'

W: 'Yes. The "cascade" of a gold colour is a firework.'

AG: 'What is that peculiar dark mark on the frame?'

W: 'It is all a part of my scheme. It balances the picture. The frame and the picture together are a work of art. The blue colouring on the gilt frame is part of the scheme of the picture; the blue spot on the right side of the frame is my monogram.'

Arrangement in Grey and Black, No. 2:
Portrait of Thomas Carlyle, 1872–3

171 × 143.5 cm. Glasgow Art Gallery and Museum

The portrait of the Scots historian and philosopher Thomas Carlyle shares the essential structure of *Arrangement in Grey and Black: Portrait of the Artist's Mother* which Whistler had painted in 1871. Carlyle had seen it in the company of Mme Venturi, who persuaded him to sit to Whistler the following year. Clearly, in the resemblance between the portraits of the two Scots there was more than can be explained by merely the superficial repetition of a successful formula. Whistler was drawn to both sitters, the first through the natural intimacy of kinship, the second for his poetic and rhetorical use of language (which Whistler often captures in his own writing), as well as for his anti-utilitarian spirit. If Whistler distorted Carlyle's ideas for his own ends, in his pronouncements concerning the ethics of work exemplified by 'Proposition No. 2', which begins, 'Industry in Art is a necessity', and concludes, 'for work alone will efface the footsteps of work', there can be no denying the vehemently austere tone echoing the Protestant spirit of Carlyle's denunciatory *angst*. In 1891 Whistler wrote revealingly about his interpretation of the subject, 'He is a favourite of mine. I like the gentle sadness about him! – perhaps he was even sensitive – and even misunderstood – who knows!' Except for the portrait studies of Carlyle by the photographer Julia Margaret Cameron – which Whistler may have known – no other nineteenth-century artist captured the sad likeness of Carlyle with as much intellectual intensity as Whistler did.

Nocturne: Blue and Silver – Battersea Reach, 1872/8

39.4 × 62.9 cm. Isabella Stewart Gardner Museum, Boston

The subject of this nocturne, the industrial Battersea shore, with Battersea Reach upstream to the right, is basically the view as seen from Chelsea outside Whistler's house in Lindsey Row. The illuminated clock tower, one hundred feet high, was built on the site of Morgan's Crucible Works in 1862, and known as 'Morgan's Folly'.

Maud Franklin, c. 1875

62.2 × 41 cm. Fogg Art Museum, Cambridge, MA

According to Margaret MacDonald, Maud Franklin, the daughter of a cabinetmaker and upholsterer, was born in Bicester, near Oxford, on 9 January 1857. If, as seems probable, she was standing in as model for *Symphony in Flesh Colour and Pink: Portrait of Mrs Frances Leyland* in 1872, she would then have been only 15, 23 years younger than Whistler. In the present portrait she may be in her mid to late teens. In the later 1870s she posed to Whistler for several etchings and portraits, perhaps the most striking being *Arrangement in White and Black* (p. 99), which was shown at the Grosvenor Gallery in 1878. She had two daughters by Whistler, one, Ióne, probably born in 1877, a second, registered as Maud McNeill Whistler Franklin, born on 13 February 1879. Maud was frequently ill in the 1880s, from which period date a number of small sketches and watercolours of her in bed. MacDonald suspects that there was at least one more pregnancy before she and Whistler finally parted. Maud accompanied Whistler to Venice in 1879–80. She showed three still-lifes at the Grosvenor Gallery exhibition of 1884, under the name 'Clifton Lin', and exhibited works at the Society of British Artists during the period of Whistler's membership. A small self-portrait, painted in a Whistlerian manner, is all that survives, but Mortimer Menpes 'thought her work very fine. She had no academic training, but we placed her high because she painted on grey panels and in sympathy with Whistler'. After Whistler married Beatrice Godwin in 1888, Maud lived in Paris, and saw much of Whistler's erstwhile friend, the Baltimore collector George Lucas, who ended his friendship with him over what he considered to be Whistler's poor treatment of Maud. She married an American, Richard H.S. Abbott, and lived near Cannes until her death, probably in 1941. She spurned all approaches from Whistler's biographers for information concerning her relationship with him.

Nocturne: Grey and Gold – Westminster Bridge, 1871/4

47 × 62.3 cm. The Burrell Collection, Glasgow Museums and Art Galleries

This subject, showing the river and the foreshortened side of the Houses of Parliament seen from Westminster Bridge, is the only picture Whistler is known to have painted of this section of the Thames. One of the 'Thames Set' etchings, however, shows the bridge, and in 1862 he painted a view of the rebuilding of Westminster Bridge, *The Last of Old Westminster* (Museum of Fine Arts, Boston), which was exhibited at the Royal Academy in 1863. In 1874 Whistler told Alfred Chapman, the managing director of a Lancashire engineering works and a collector of his paintings, that he had 'just the picture for you – a hundred pounder – A very warm summer night on the Thames – lovely in colour they say – a Nocturne in blue and gold – view of the river from the Houses of Parliament'. The picture was first exhibited at the Dudley Gallery in 1875, where it was bought by Percy Wyndham for £210. At the Ruskin trial, after it had been shown in the 1877 Grosvenor Gallery exhibition, Whistler cited the sale in evidence, and complained that since Ruskin's criticism he had been unable to get a comparable price for his pictures.

Cremorne Gardens, No. 2, 1875

68.5 × 134.9 cm. Metropolitan Museum of Art, New York

Whistler made six nocturnal paintings of Cremorne Gardens in Chelsea; this is the largest. They probably all date from the summer or autumn of 1875, or just after, since *Nocturne in Black and Gold: The Falling Rocket* was first shown in the Dudley Gallery in November of that year. From the early 1870s, Cremorne was the subject of much local hostility, because of the level of noise and immorality that it engendered. On several occasions the local authority withheld a licence for music and dancing. For this reason profits declined, the gardens were sold in 1877, and houses built on the site. The clientèle of Cremorne was characterized by one contemporary commentator thus: 'Dukes and duchesses, at least not openly, did not frequent it . . . but it was more essentially the resort of middle-class youth, of medical students, Oxonians, Cantabs, provincials up on holiday, and the gay sisterhood, though among the frequenters were to be found tradesmen and their wives and respectable actresses, who came for the shows and not for the fun.' Here Whistler presents an unspecific rendering of Cremorne's *habitués* and their activities, relieved only by the artificial lighting and a corner of the dancing platform. Similar subjects had been treated, with greater social differentiation, by English artists and illustrators, and by the French Impressionists, but Whistler preferred instead the anonymity of darkness to mask the social relationships and add a sense of mystery to what would otherwise be an essentially mundane subject.

Arrangement in Brown and Black: Miss Rosa Corder, 1876–8

192.4 × 92.4 cm. Frick Collection, New York

The artist Rosa Corder was the mistress of the art dealer and entrepreneur Charles Augustus Howell, who assisted Whistler in selling his art, particularly his prints, in the late 1870s. She seems to have become embroiled in Howell's affairs, not only as mother to his child, but also as a copyist, probably even as a fabricator of Rossetti drawings. Whistler's portrait of her was commissioned by Howell for £100; he told Whistler he could expect further proceeds from the sale of mezzotint engravings of it, which were published in 1880. According to Whistler, when the portrait was half done Howell paid him £70 out of money advanced to him by H. Graves and Company on a proposed portrait by Whistler of Disraeli, which was never painted; or rather, Howell paid him out of money Whistler had just lent him. When the portrait was exhibited at the Grosvenor Gallery in 1879 it drew a generally sympathetic response from critics, some of whom compared it, favourably, with Velázquez. After Howell's death in 1892 it was bought by the artist Graham Robertson, who invited Whistler to come and see it again. In his memoirs Robertson describes their reunion. 'The meeting between the painter and his masterpiece, *Rosa Corder*, was quite touching. He hung over her, he breathed softly upon her surface and gently stroked her with his handkerchief, he dusted her delicately and lovingly. "*Isn't* she beautiful," he said – and so she was.'

Nocturne in Black and Gold: The Falling Rocket, 1875

60.3 × 46.6 cm. Detroit Institute of Arts

This nocturne, exhibited at the Grosvenor Gallery in 1877, was the principal target of Ruskin's criticism when he accused Whistler of 'flinging a pot of paint in the public's face'. At the trial for libel, Ruskin's counsel, the Attorney-General, Sir John Holker, asked Whistler:

'Did it take you much time to paint the Nocturne in black and gold; how soon did you knock it off?' (laughter)

W: 'I beg your pardon.'

AG: 'I was using an expression which was rather more appropriate to my own profession.' (laughter)

W: 'Thank you for the compliment' (a laugh)

AG: 'How long do you take to knock off one of your pictures?'

W: 'Oh, I knock one off possibly in a couple of days (laughter) – one day to do the work, and another to finish it. The Nocturne in black and gold was done in a day, completed on the second' . . .

AG: 'And that was the labour for which you asked 200 guineas?'

W: 'No, it was for the knowledge gained through a lifetime.' (applause)

Later, Whistler was again cross-examined by the Attorney-General: 'You have made the study of art your study of a lifetime. What is the peculiar beauty of that picture?'

W: 'It is impossible for me to explain to you the beauty of the picture, any more than for a musician to explain to you the beauty of harmony in a particular piece of music if you had no ear for music. I could make it clear to any sympathetic painter, but I do not think I could to you. I have known unbiased people, comparatively ignorant of art, express the opinion that it represents fireworks in a night sky.'

AG: 'Do you think that anybody looking at the picture might fairly come to the conclusion that it had no peculiar beauty?'

W: 'I have strong evidence that Mr Ruskin came to the conclusion that there was no particular beauty in the picture.'

AG: 'Do you think it fair that Mr Ruskin should come to that conclusion?'

W: 'What might be fair to Mr Ruskin I can't answer. No artist of culture would come to that conclusion.'

Arrangement in White and Black, c. 1876

191.4 × 90.9 cm. Freer Gallery of Art, Washington DC

This painting, a portrait of Maud Franklin, was exhibited at the Grosvenor Gallery in 1878. Whistler depicts Maud in the slim skirts of an out-of-doors walking costume which was then very fashionable. Margaret MacDonald has pointed out that the costume echoes the one described in the fashion column of the *Graphic* on 4 May 1878: 'White sateen will be much worn, more or less trimmed with coloured ribbons . . . those whose features are irregular . . . can disguise their high foreheads with light curls, fringes, etc . . . Bonnets and hats are very graceful at the present time. White or black, whether in silk, satin or tulle, form dress-bonnets and hats.' The coquettish pose, and the emphasis on up-to-date fashion, relate Whistler's portrait to some of Manet's, especially his portrait of the actress Ellen Andrée as *La Parisienne*, also of 1876 (Nationalmuseum, Stockholm).

Harmony in Blue: The Duet, c. 1878

27.3 × 45.7 cm. Rhode Island School of Design, Providence, RI

Although Whistler was interested in the theatre, even performing himself in amateur productions in the 1870s, he seldom represented the stage in his art. A portrait of the skipping-rope dancer Connie Gilchrist, *Harmony in Yellow and Gold*, and *Arrangement in Black, No. 3: Sir Henry Irving as Philip II of Spain* (both Metropolitan Museum of Art, New York) are his only known paintings of theatrical performers, although he represented Lady Archibald Campbell (see p. 109) as Orlando in *As You Like It* staged in the grounds of Coombe Woods, Kingston, in 1884. He was often at the Gaiety Theatre, and attended performances of the *Grasshopper*, Hollingshead's adaptation of Meilhac and Halévy's *La Cigale*, first produced in Paris, in which Degas and his art were satirized. In the London production, Whistler was the target, and a life-size cartoon of him by Pellegrini appeared on stage. In October 1877 Whistler made pen drawings of the Gaiety burlesque, *Little Dr Faust*, by H.J. Byron. In January 1878 he expressed the wish to paint the star of the show, Nellie Farren. It is possible that *Harmony in Blue: The Duet* relates to this production. Appropriately, this theatrical scene, in artificial light, is reminiscent of Degas's stage subjects.

The Gold Scab, 1879

186.7 × 137 cm. Fine Arts Museums of San Francisco

Whistler painted three pictures satirizing F.R. Leyland; two others, *The Loves of the Lobsters* and *Mount Ararat*, have not survived. He probably intended all three to be in his studio when Leyland and the creditors made an inspection of the White House in 1879. Whistler blamed Leyland for his refusal to pay him the £2000 he had asked for decorating the Peacock Room in 1876–7, which (among other factors) resulted in his having to sell the White House and his ultimate bankruptcy in May 1879. *The Gold Scab* shows Leyland as a hideous peacock sitting on Whistler's White House, playing the piano. Leyland's money and his addiction to frilled shorts are the subject of especial derision. Inscribed on the music score are the words: 'THE "Gold Scab". Eruption in FRiLthy Lucre!' Ironically, the painting has a decorated frame, bearing the first bars from the third movement of Schubert's *Moments Musicaux*, Opus 94. It was originally intended to frame the enlargement of the 'Three Girls' composition Leyland had commissioned, but which Whistler probably destroyed at about this time. Of Whistler and *The Gold Scab* Arthur Symons wrote: 'He was a great master of the grotesque in conversation, and the portrait which he made of Mr Leyland as a many-tentacled devil at a piano, a thing of horror and beauty, is for once a verbal image put into paint, with that wholehearted delight in exuberant extravagance which made his talk wildly heroic. That painting is his one joke in paint, his one expression of a personal feeling so violent that it overcame his scruples as an artist. And yet even that is not really an exception; for out of a malicious joke, begun, certainly, in anger, beauty exudes like the scent of a poisonous flower.'

Winter Evening, 1880

30 × 20.2 cm. Freer Gallery of Art, Washington DC

Winter Evening was shown in the exhibition of Venetian pastels at the Fine Art Society, London, in 1881. Whistler's minimal use of colour, in which much of the brown paper is left exposed to create the atmospheric suggestion of a winter night, makes this one of the most sophisticated of the pastels he made in Venice in 1880. Otto Bacher described his methods: 'He generally selected bits of strange architecture, windows, piles, balconies, queer water effects, canal views with boats – very rarely figure subjects – always little artistic views that would not be complete in any other medium . . . In beginning a pastel he drew his subject crisply and carefully in outline with black crayon upon one of those sheets of tinted paper which fitted the general colour of the motive. A few touches with sky-tinted pastels, corresponding to nature, produced a remarkable effect, with touches of reds, greys, and yellows for the buildings here and there. The reflections of the sky and houses upon the water finished the work.'

Nocturne in Blue and Silver: The Lagoon, Venice, 1879/80

51 × 66 cm. Museum of Fine Arts, Boston

Whistler made few oil paintings in Venice, concentrating instead on etchings and pastels. Although he wrote to Alfred Chapman in 1878, 'If I go to Venice would you like to go in for a Nocturne of the Gondola kind?', a *Nocturne in Blue and Gold* of St Mark's in the National Museum of Wales, Cardiff, and this *Nocturne in Blue and Silver*, which shows the Church of San Giorgio, are all that survive. In Venice Whistler preferred to etch nocturnes, translating into another medium what he had already achieved in paint.

Arrangement in Black: The Lady in the Yellow Buskin – Portrait of Lady Archibald Campbell, 1882–4

213.3 × 109.2 cm. Philadelphia Museum of Art

Janey Sevilla Callander of Craigforth, Stirling, and Ardkinglass, Argyll, married the second son of the eighth Duke of Argyll in 1869. Her patronage significantly assisted Whistler's position in London society after his return from Venice in 1880. In her turn, Lady Archibald was much influenced by Whistler's colour theories, as expressed in her book *Rainbow Music or The Philosophy of Harmony in Colour-Grouping*, published in 1886. Whistler painted three portraits of her, one in black velvet court-dress; a second as *The Grey Lady*, a 'harmony in silver greys' which gave 'the impression of movement . . . descending the steps of a stair'; and this, the only one to survive. She described Whistler asking her to pose for it 'in the dress in which I called upon him'. The portrait was not a commission. The Campbell family rejected it 'with the delicate remark that it represented a street walker encouraging a shy follower with a backward glance'. The unusual blend of the aristocracy and the *demi-monde* made such comments inevitable when it was shown at the Salon of 1885. Degas greatly admired it, and said, 'She is going back into the cave of Watteau.' Huysmans described her as retreating 'into black shadows which are both deep and warm; two strokes of tinder brown – her little shoes and the long gloves she is buttoning up ring out through the darkness where the shadows lift a little towards the bottom of the canvas; but that is a mere accessory, a detail taking its place in the whole intended by the painter . . . the artist has drawn forth, from the flesh, an elusive expression of the soul, and he has also transmuted his model into a disquieting sphinx.'

An Orange Note: Sweet Shop, 1884

12.2 × 21.5 cm. Freer Gallery of Art, Washington DC

This picture was painted either at St Ives, Cornwall, in the winter of 1883–4, or shortly after in Chelsea. It is typical of the small shop-fronts Whistler painted in Chelsea, Dieppe and Holland in the 1880s; several of them were shown in the two exhibitions 'Notes – Harmonies – Nocturnes', held by the Dowdeswell Gallery, London, in 1884 and 1886. A description which appeared in a review of the 1884 exhibition, in the *Standard*, suggests the appeal of what he left out, as much as the expressive manner of the little that he put in. 'The shop is probably the most perfect little thing of its kind that was ever wrought by an artist who has learnt to see . . . It is without detail, without apparent labour, without dramatic interest, but it is exquisite in colour, faultless in tone, and its well considered mystery has, at least, the interest of suggestiveness.' Together with a landscape of the same size, it was bought from the exhibition for £160, by Wickham Flower.

Arrangement in Flesh Colour and Black: Portrait of Théodore Duret, 1883–4

193.4 × 90.8 cm. Metropolitan Museum of Art, New York

The art critic Théodore Duret had been introduced to Whistler by Manet in 1880. He owned several of Whistler's paintings, and published a number of influential articles on him, as well as a monograph (1904). In his review of modern English art in 1881 Duret had written: 'M. Whistler leads the way.' At the time that Whistler was painting his portrait Duret was often in London, having been commissioned by the *Gazette des Beaux-Arts* to review the London exhibitions, particularly those of the Grosvenor Gallery, where Whistler exhibited until 1884. It was after a visit they had made there in 1883, when Whistler had criticized the portrait of a corporation president painted with a contemporary haircut but dressed in an antique-style robe, that he decided to paint Duret in modern evening dress. He asked Duret to pose carrying a pink domino mask, which the critic found at a theatrical costumer's in Covent Garden. He posed repeatedly in 1883–4, the canvas being completely repainted at least ten times. Each time, according to Duret, Whistler attacked the canvas without any preliminary drawing. He first put in a few light touches of chalk to indicate where the head would go at the top, the feet at the bottom, and the position of the body, to left and right. He immediately applied the colours and tones on to the canvas as they would be in the finished picture. At the end of the first sitting the general physiognomy of the portrait could already be judged. When Duret showed the portrait to visitors in his apartment in Paris, he would, according to Pennell, 'take a sheet of paper, cut a hole in it, and place it against the background, to prove that the grey, when surrounded by white, is pure and cold, without a touch of rose, and that Whistler got his effect by his knowledge of the relation of colours, and his mastery of the tones he wished to obtain'.

Grey and Silver: Mist – Life Boat, 1884

12.3 × 21.6 cm. Freer Gallery of Art, Washington DC

This was probably painted at St Ives, Cornwall, in the winter of 1883/4. With Whistler at this time were the 'Followers', the artists Walter Sickert and Mortimer Menpes, who, like him, painted on wood panels of a similarly small size. The red on the lifeboat, which is picked up in one woman's shawl and in the butterfly, provides a good example of Whistler's use of his signature to co-ordinate the colour scheme. This little panel was a particularly well-travelled one. After being shown in Dowdeswell's 1884 exhibition, it travelled to Dublin; then to Georges Petit's gallery in Paris, in 1887; to Munich in 1888; to New York in 1889; and finally to Brussels in 1890, where it was bought by the violinist Pablo Sarasate's manager, Otto Gold-schmidt, for £200.

White and Grey: The Hotel Courtyard, Dieppe, 1885

21.7 × 12.5 cm. Fogg Art Museum, Cambridge, MA

In September 1885 Whistler stayed with Walter Sickert and his wife in Dieppe, where they had recently rented a house. In Dieppe Whistler painted about a dozen oils, some of which, including this one, were shown in his second exhibition of 'Notes – Harmonies – Nocturnes' at Dowdeswell's Gallery, London, in May 1886. It was then exhibited in Munich in 1888 and in New York in 1889, before being bought by the Scots collector J.J. Cowan from the Glasgow dealer Alexander Reid, for £90.

Blue and Violet: La Belle de Jour, c. 1885

17.2 × 10.8 cm. Fogg Art Museum, Cambridge, MA

Whistler explained to the first owner of this small panel that 'belle de jour' was a blue and violet flower, which colour scheme he took for the picture. Its subject is typical of the many figure subjects, more often in pastel than in oil, which Whistler made in the later 1880s and 1890s. It recapitulates the neo-classical studies of female nudes which he made in the late 1860s and early 1870s.

Chelsea Shop, 1887/90

12.4 × 21.5 cm. Rhode Island School of Design, Providence

Once the Chelsea Embankment was opened in 1874, a number of shops which had previously been hidden from sight by the waterfront that was demolished to build it came into more prominent view. Shops such as this one – the vegetables on and under the table suggest a greengrocer's – had once been red-brick domestic houses of the seventeenth and eighteenth centuries. They were in stark and old-fashioned contrast to the streamlined modernism of the granite-faced Embankment which swept by in front of them. As the modernization of Chelsea continued in the 1880s, with large apartment blocks built to house the rapidly expanding parish, little premises like this one would soon be demolished to make way for new developments – which in his art Whistler never showed.

Harmony in Fawn Colour and Purple:
Portrait of Miss Milly Finch, c. 1885

189.3 × 88.7 cm. Hunterian Art Gallery, Glasgow

Whistler painted three related portraits of the model Milly Finch. The other two, one in *Coral and Blue*, another in *Blue and Violet*, are also in the Hunterian Art Gallery. They are unfinished and would have been considered unsuitable for showing in a large public exhibition in the nineteenth century. Nevertheless, their spectral harmonies of colour, bravura brushwork, and vivacious expression now make them intensely appealing. The apparent spontaneity is revealing of the ambition Whistler had for his later portraits; due to his prolonged labour at the canvas, it was not always preserved to the end. There are many recorded instances of Whistler being implored, by friends and sitters alike, not to 'improve' what he had already achieved so well. But with the three portraits of Milly Finch, which were in his studio when he died, he seems to have had no need for such advice. Even Manet would have envied them.

Flower Market, Dieppe, 1885

12.8 × 21 cm. Freer Gallery of Art, Washington DC

Although Whistler had used watercolour on his Rhine journey in 1858, which resulted in the 'French Set' etchings, it was not until the 1880s that it became a medium he used regularly for seascapes, shop-fronts, and subjects such as this one. The *Flower Market, Dieppe* was painted when Whistler was in the town in September 1885, and given to Walter Sickert, with whom he was then staying. It is typical of other exuberant watercolours and small-scale oils, also of Dieppe, which were shown in his second exhibition of 'Notes – Harmonies – Nocturnes' at Dowdeswell's Gallery in 1886.

London Bridge, 1885

17.5 × 27.8 cm. Freer Gallery of Art, Washington DC

An article by Sickert in *Truth* for 7 May 1885 identifies *London Bridge* as the watercolour *Grey and Silver: London* shown at the Society of British Artists' spring exhibition of 1885. The luminous tones of *London Bridge* recall Turner. Although Whistler reviled Turner, he was never afraid to tackle similar subjects, whether in Venice or London. In doing so he substituted his own severer geometry and 'scientific' use of colour for what he always thought was lacking in Turner's work.

The Grey House, 1889

23.5 × 13.8 cm. Freer Gallery of Art, Washington DC

In Amsterdam in September 1889 Whistler concentrated on etchings. He produced a few watercolours, but only two oils are recorded: one of a canal, and this, *The Grey House*, which resembles the composition of one of his most elaborate etchings of Amsterdam, *The Embroidered Curtain* (K. 410). The same scene also appears in the etching *Jews' Quarter, Amsterdam* (K. 415).

Annabel Lee, c. 1890

32.3 × 18 cm. Freer Gallery of Art, Washington DC

This pastel on brown paper, which also goes under the name *Niobe* – the legendary queen who was turned to stone while mourning her children – dates from about 1890. Its conception, however, perhaps even its actual beginning, relates to a figure in *Variations in Blue and Green*, which was one of the six oil sketches Whistler made for F.R. Leyland in 1868. Whether *Niobe* or *Annabel Lee*, named after the poem of Edgar Allan Poe – the subject of which Whistler also painted in the late 1860s – the figure's mood and evocative colouring is as appropriate to the Symbolist milieu of Mallarmé, of which Whistler was an integral part in 1890, as it is to the period when his friendship with Swinburne was at its height.

Arrangement in Flesh Colour and Brown: Portrait of Arthur J. Eddy, 1894

209.9 × 92.4 cm. The Art Institute of Chicago

The Chicago lawyer Arthur Jerome Eddy was an early collector in America of cubist and abstract art. He commissioned his portrait from Whistler in 1893, and it was painted in six weeks in his studio in the rue Notre-Dame-des-Champs, Paris, in 1894. In his book *Recollections and Impressions of James A. McNeill Whistler* (1903), Eddy described his progress with the portrait:

'He worked with great rapidity and long hours, but he used his colors thin and covered the canvas with innumerable coats of paint. The colors increased in depth and intensity as the work progressed. At first the entire figure was painted in grayish-brown tones, with very little flesh color, the whole blending perfectly with the grayish-brown of the prepared canvas; then the entire background would be intensified a little; then the figure made a little stronger; then the background, and so on from day to day and week to week, and often from month to month, to the exhaustion of the sitter, but the perfection of the work, if the sitter remained patient and continued in favor.

'At no time did he permit the figure to get away from or out of the background; at no time did he permit the background to oppress the figure, but the development of both was even and harmonious, with neither discord nor undue contrast.

'And so the portrait would really grow, really develop as an entirety, very much as a negative under the action of the chemicals comes out gradually – lights, shadows, and all from the first faint indications to their full values.

'It was as if the portrait were hidden within the canvas and the master by passing his wands day after day over the surface evoked the image.'

Miss Rosalind Birnie Philip Standing, c. 1897

23.4 × 13.7 cm. Hunterian Art Gallery, Glasgow

Rosalind, the daughter of the sculptor John Birnie Philip, was 22 when her eldest sister Beatrice, Whistler's wife, died in 1896. Whistler then made her his ward and executrix; she acted as his secretary until his death in 1903. Thereafter she became something of a jealous guardian of Whistler's memory. Believing that Whistler never wanted his biography written, she prevented the Pennells quoting from Whistler's letters in their book on him, published in 1908. She also dissociated herself from the memorial exhibition of Whistler's work planned by Pennell and the Council of the International Society of Sculptors, Painters and Gravers, and shown in London in 1905. She collaborated instead with the Whistler collector, Charles Lang Freer of Detroit, and lent works to the memorial exhibition which was held in Paris in the same year. She presented an important group of paintings and drawings to the University of Glasgow in 1935, and followed this up, in 1955 and 1958, with a bequest which consisted of the rest of the Whistler estate, including some 6000 letters, ledgers, books, catalogues, press cuttings, and other memorabilia. She posed for several drawings and lithographs by him, as well as five paintings, three of which are now in the Hunterian Art Gallery. The present portrait was painted in the drawing-room of 110 Rue du Bac in about 1897.

Portrait of Charles Lang Freer, 1902

51.8 × 31.7 cm. Freer Gallery of Art, Washington DC

Charles Lang Freer was born in Kingston, New York, in 1856. In partnership with Colonel Frank J. Hecker he founded the Peninsular Car Works in Detroit, which produced railway rolling stock. After forming the American Car and Foundry Company he was able to retire from business in 1900, and devote himself exclusively to art collecting. He began to collect Whistler's etchings in 1887, and after meeting Whistler in 1890, set out, with single-minded determination and the appropriate financial resources, to form the largest single collection of his work anywhere. He was known principally as a pioneering collector of the art of the Far East and Asia; his friendship with Whistler was instrumental in influencing the formation of his taste. On his death in 1919 he bequeathed to the American nation his Oriental and Whistler collections – comprising some 70 oil paintings, and works in other media, including *The Peacock Room* – together with paintings by Whistler's American contemporaries. They are now displayed in the Freer Gallery of Art, in the Smithsonian Institution, Washington DC, which opened to the public in 1923.

Brown and Gold (Self-Portrait), 1895/1900

95.8 × 51.5 cm. Hunterian Art Gallery, Glasgow

Whistler based the pose of this late self-portrait on that of Velázquez's *Pablo de Valladolid* in the Prado, Madrid, of which he owned a photograph. Progress on it was interrupted by his wife's illness and death. Its unflattering pathos undoubtedly reflects these events. It is also an enduring testimony to Velázquez's lasting influence on Whistler, who, throughout his career, like Manet, adopted the pose for several of his full-length portraits. It was shown in the American section of the Paris Exposition Universelle of 1900, when Whistler was awarded the *Grand Prix*. The critic Gustave Geffroy described it as 'vague like an apparition, but so gripping, so real'. Whistler regretted its exhibition and stated, 'It was not ready, the colour has sunk in, you cannot see it, and really it is very swagger.' After the exhibition he rubbed the portrait down but did not repaint it.

SELECT BIBLIOGRAPHY

Reference and Standard Catalogues of Whistler's Work

GETSCHER, Robert H. and MARKS, Paul G., *James McNeill Whistler and John Singer Sargent, Two Annotated Bibliographies*, Garland Publishing Inc., New York and London, 1986.

YOUNG, Andrew McLaren, MACDONALD, Margaret, SPENCER, Robin and MILES, Hamish, *The Paintings of James McNeill Whistler*, Yale University Press, 2 vols., New Haven and London, 1980.

KENNEDY, Edward G., *The Etched Work of Whistler, Illustrated by Reproductions in Collotype of the Different States of the Plates*, New York, 1910 (new edition, Alan Wofsy Fine Arts, San Francisco, 1978).

WAY, Thomas R., *Mr. Whistler's Lithographs. The Catalogue, compiled by T.R. Way*, G. Bell and Sons, London, 2nd edition, 1905 (new edition, *Whistler's Lithographs, A Catalogue Raisonné* by Mervyn Levy, Jupiter Books, London, 1975).

WHISTLER, James McNeill, *The Gentle Art of Making Enemies*, William Heinemann and G.P. Putnam, London and New York, 1892 (and subsequent editions).

Monographs

BACHER, Otto, *With Whistler in Venice*, The Century Company, New York, 1908.

DURET, Théodore, *Histoire de J. McN. Whistler et de son oeuvre*, H. Floury, Paris, 1904.

FINE, Ruth E., *James McNeill Whistler, A Reexamination*, Studies in the History of Art, vol. 19, Washington, 1987.

MENPES, Mortimer, *Whistler as I Knew Him*, Adam and Charles Black, London, 1904.

PENNELL, Elizabeth Robins and Joseph, *The Life of James McNeill Whistler*, 2 vols., William Heinemann and J.B. Lippincott Company, London and Philadelphia, 1908.

PENNELL, Elizabeth Robins and Joseph, *The Whistler Journal*, J.B. Lippincott Company, Philadelphia, 1921.

SPENCER, Robin, *Whistler A Retrospective*, Hugh Lauter Levin Associates, Inc., New York, 1989.

SUTTON, Denys, *Nocturne: The Art of James McNeill Whistler*, Country Life Ltd., London, 1963.

TAYLOR, Hilary, *James McNeill Whistler*, Studio Vista, London, 1978.

WAY, T.R., *Memories of James McNeill Whistler*, John Lane, London and New York, 1912.

CHRONOLOGY

1834
July 11. James Abbott Whistler is born in Lowell, Massachusetts.

1843–1848
Mrs Whistler, her two sons James and William and stepdaughter Deborah, join Major Whistler in St Petersburg. Whistler attends drawing lessons at the Imperial Academy of Fine Arts.

1849
Stays with the Hadens in London, and then lives in Pomfret, Connecticut.

1851
Enters West Point Military Academy.

1854
Discharged from West Point for deficiency in chemistry. Works as an apprentice at Ross Winans' locomotive works in Baltimore, and is then appointed to drawing division of the United States Coast and Geodetic Survey, Washington DC.

1855
Arrives in Paris and enters the studio of Charles Gleyre. Meets Du Maurier, Armstrong, Poynter and other English artists.

1857
Visits Art Treasures exhibition in Manchester.

1858
On an etching tour of northern France, Luxembourg and the Rhineland, publishes the 'French Set'. Formation of the 'Société de Trois': Fantin, Whistler and Legros.

1859
His painting praised by Courbet. Moves to London, staying with the Hadens and in rooms in Wapping. Begins the 'Thames Set' series of etchings.

1860
At the Piano exhibited at the R.A. Joanna Hiffernan becomes his mistress and principal model.

1861
Visits Brittany. In Paris, painting *The White Girl*, later called *Symphony in White, No. 1: The White Girl*.

1862
Thames etchings exhibited in Paris and praised by Baudelaire. *The White Girl* rejected by the R.A. Paints seascapes at Guéthary, Basses-Pyrénées.

1863

Moves to 7 Lindsey Row in Chelsea near Rossetti. *The White Girl* at the Salon des Refusés. Whistler's mother comes to live with him.

1864

Poses with Manet, Baudelaire and others for Fantin's *Homage to Delacroix*.

1865

His brother, Dr William Whistler, comes to live in London. Albert Moore replaces Legros in the 'Société de Trois'.

1866

Travels to South America and witnesses the Chilean war of liberation against Spain.

1867

Moves to 2 Lindsey Row, Chelsea. Accuses Seymour Haden of disrespect towards his late partner, Dr Traer, and violently assaults Haden in Paris. Writes to Fantin-Latour rejecting Courbet's realism, and wishing he could have studied under Ingres. Expelled from the Burlington Fine Art Club as a result of the Haden affair.

1870

Birth of Charles Whistler Hanson, child of Whistler and Louisa Hanson, a parlourmaid.

1871

Publishes *Sixteen Etchings of Scenes on the Thames* and begins to paint a succession of Thames nocturnes. Paints the portrait of his mother, *Arrangement in Grey and Black*. Begins to exhibit work in small London dealers' exhibitions.

1872

Arrangement in Grey and Black: Portrait of the Artist's Mother is admitted to the R.A., the last picture shown there by Whistler.

1873

Begins to give dinner parties and initiates his midday 'Sunday breakfasts'. Maud Franklin takes Jo's place as Whistler's mistress and chief model.

1874

Holds his first one-man exhibition, in the Flemish Gallery, Pall Mall.

1875

Mrs Whistler retires to Hastings. Painting Nocturnes of Cremorne Gardens in Chelsea including *Nocturne in Black and Gold: The Falling Rocket* which is exhibited at the Dudley Gallery in November.

1877

Completes the Peacock Room for F.R. Leyland which Whistler calls *Harmony in Blue and Gold*. Sues Ruskin for libel in respect of his criticism of *The Falling Rocket* exhibited at the Grosvenor Gallery.

1878

Moves to the White House, Tite Street, Chelsea. Awarded a farthing's damages without costs in his libel action against Ruskin, and publishes *Whistler v. Ruskin: Art and Art Critics*.

1879

Maud has a child, Maud McNeill Whistler Franklin. Auction sale of Whistler's possessions. Declared bankrupt. Bailiffs take possession of the White House, which is then sold. Leaves for Venice with Maud, and a commission from The Fine Art Society for twelve etchings.

1880

Sale of his effects at Sotheby's. Returns to London and stays with his brother until he finds lodgings. Introduced to Duret by Manet.

1881

Whistler's mother dies at Hastings. He paints seascapes in Jersey and Guernsey. Leases flat and studio at 13 Tite Street. Becomes friendly with Oscar Wilde.

1882

Portrait of Lady Meux and three Venice etchings are exhibited at the Salon. Walter Sickert leaves the Slade School of Art to become Whistler's pupil and assistant.

1883

Whistler in Paris. At the Salon the portrait of his mother is awarded a third-class medal, and enthusiastically reviewed by Théodore Duret. Paintings exhibited at the Galerie Georges Petit. Painting oils and watercolours in Holland.

1884

At St Ives, Cornwall, with his pupils Mortimer Menpes and W.R. Sickert. Painting small seascapes. First exhibition with the Société des XX, Brussels. In Holland around Dordrecht painting and etching. Exhibits his portraits of Cicely Alexander and Carlyle at the Salon. Opening of one-man exhibition, *Notes – Harmonies – Nocturnes*, at Dowdeswell's, London. Meets Joseph Pennell, his future biographer. Leases studio at 454A Fulham Road. Elected member of the Society of British Artists.

1885

Delivers the 'Ten O'Clock' lecture in Princes Hall. Portraits of Lady Archibald Campbell and Duret are exhibited at the Salon. Visits Belgium and Holland.

1886

Set of Twenty-Six Etchings of Venice are issued by Dowdeswell's in London. Second one-man exhibition, *Notes – Harmonies – Nocturnes*, at Dowdeswell's. Exhibits the portrait of Sarasate at the Paris Salon and in Brussels. Elected president of the S.B.A.

1887
Oils, watercolours and pastels are exhibited at the Galerie Georges Petit in Paris. The Society of British Artists receives a Royal Charter, thus becoming the Royal Society of British Artists (R.B.A.). Visits Holland and Belgium with Dr and Mrs Whistler.

1888
Exhibits nocturnes, etchings and drawings at the Galerie Durand-Ruel in Paris. Resigns as president of the R.B.A. Menpes, Sickert, Alfred Stevens, Théodore Roussel and others also resign. Monet introduces Whistler to Stéphane Mallarmé who agrees to translate the 'Ten O'Clock' lecture into French. Moves to the Tower House, Tite Street. Sends oils and a group of watercolours, pastels and etchings to the third Internationale Kunst-Ausstellung in Munich, and is awarded a second-class medal. Marries Beatrice Godwin, widow of E.W. Godwin; working honeymoon in France.

1889
Big exhibition of his oils, watercolours and pastels held at Wunderlich's in New York. Banquet for Whistler in Paris is followed by a dinner in London to celebrate the award of a first-class medal at Munich and the Cross of St Michael of Bavaria. Makes etchings in Amsterdam. Awarded a gold medal at the International Exhibition in Amsterdam and made a Chevalier of the Légion d'Honneur.

1890
Moves to 21 Cheyne Walk. Meets C.L. Freer of Detroit, who forms a major collection of Whistler's work. Exhibits two nocturnes at the Paris Salon and several paintings at the Brussels Salon. *The Gentle Art of Making Enemies* is published in London by Heinemann.

1891
The Corporation of Glasgow buys the portrait of Carlyle. Whistler's portrait of his mother is bought for the Musée du Luxembourg.

1892
Important retrospective exhibition, *Nocturnes, Marines & Chevalet Pieces*, at the Goupil Gallery in London. Moves to a house at 110 Rue du Bac, Paris.

1895
Sir William Eden brings an action against Whistler for not handing over the portrait of Lady Eden. Judgment goes against Whistler. Working on etchings, lithographs and paintings, in Lyme Regis.

1896
J.S. Sargent lends Whistler his studio. Takes studio in Fitzroy Street.

The Whistlers move to St Jude's Cottage on Hampstead Heath. Death of Mrs Whistler. He adopts his sister-in-law Rosalind Birnie Philip as his ward, and makes her his executrix. Goes to Honfleur, Dieppe and Calais.

1897
Whistler supports Pennell in his successful libel action against Sickert. In Dieppe with Pennell and E.G. Kennedy. Whistler's appeal in the case with Sir William Eden is heard in Paris. This time the verdict goes in Whistler's favour.

1898
Elected president of the International Society of Sculptors, Painters and Gravers.

1899
Visits Italy for the marriage of William Heinemann. His account of the Eden case, *Eden versus Whistler: The Baronet and the Butterfly*, is published in Paris. At Pavillon Madelaine, Pourville-sur-Mer near Dieppe with the Birnie Philips.

1900
Death of his brother William. Heinemann asks the Pennells to write the authorized life of Whistler. Visits Holland and then joins the Birnie Philips near Dublin for three weeks. He is very ill in Marseilles and then sails for Corsica.

1901
Closes the studio in Paris and sells 110 Rue du Bac. Convalesces in Bath with the Birnie Philips.

1902
Leases 72 Cheyne Walk from the architect C.R. Ashbee and lives there with the Birnie Philips. While on holiday with Freer in The Hague, Whistler becomes seriously ill. Visits Scheveningen, the Mauritshuis and galleries at Haarlem.

1903
Receives honorary degree of Doctor of Laws from the University of Glasgow but is too ill to attend the ceremony. Dies on July 17. He is buried in Chiswick Cemetery.

1904
Memorial exhibition of his work in Boston, Copley Society.

1905
About 750 works are exhibited at the memorial exhibition *Paintings, Drawings, Etchings and Lithographs* by the International Society in London, and about 440 in the Ecole des Beaux-Arts, *Oeuvres de James McNeill Whistler*, in Paris.

LIST OF PLATES

6: Sir Joseph Boehm: *Bust of Whistler*, 1875, terracotta, height 50.8 cm. Toledo Museum of Art, Toledo, Ohio (Gift of Florence Scott Libbey).

10: *The Coast Survey Plate*, 1854–5, etching (K.1), 14.9 × 26.3 cm. Freer Gallery of Art, Smithsonian Institution, Washington DC.

11: *The Title to the 'French Set'*, 1858, etching (K.25), 11.1 × 14.6 cm. Hunterian Art Gallery, University of Glasgow (J.W. Revillon Bequest).

12: *Street at Saverne*, 1858, etching (K.19 iv), 20.8 × 15.7 cm. Hunterian Art Gallery, University of Glasgow (J.W. Revillon Bequest).

15: Whistler photographed by Etienne Carjat in Paris, c. 1864. Whistler Collections, Glasgow University Library.

16: *Speke Hall No. 1*, 1870, etching and drypoint, 22.6 × 15.2 cm. Hunterian Art Gallery, University of Glasgow.

18: *The Peacock Room*, 1876–7: central shutter, east wall, oil and gold leaf on wood. Freer Gallery of Art, Smithsonian Institution, Washington DC.

21: *The Velvet Dress*, 1873, etching and drypoint (K.105 v), 23.2 × 15.8 cm. Freer Gallery of Art, Smithsonian Institution, Washington DC.

24: *The Beggars, Venice*, 1880, etching and drypoint (K.194 viii), 30.5 × 21 cm. Hunterian Art Gallery, University of Glasgow (Birnie Philip Bequest).

25: *The Little Lagoon, Venice*, 1880, etching (K.186 ii), 22.5 × 15.1 cm. Hunterian Art Gallery, University of Glasgow.

26: *Palaces, Venice*, 1880, etching and drypoint (K.187 iii), Hunterian Art Gallery, University of Glasgow (Birnie Philip Gift).

27: Whistler painting in his Fulham Road studio, photograph, 1884/8. Whistler Collections, Glasgow University Library. The portrait in the background is probably of Maud Franklin.

30: *Portrait of Mallarmé, No. 1*, 1894, lithograph (W.66), 9.5 × 7 cm. Hunterian Art Gallery, University of Glasgow (Birnie Philip Gift).

32: Whistler and Mortimer Menpes, c. 1885, photograph (reproduced from *Whistler as I Knew Him* by Mortimer Menpes, 1904).

33: *Walter Sickert*, 1895, lithograph (W.79), 19 × 14 cm. Reproduced by courtesy of the Trustees of the British Museum, London.

34: Sheet of drypoints of Whistler by Mortimer Menpes, c. 1885 (reproduced from *Whistler as I Knew Him* by Mortimer Menpes, 1904).

36: *La Belle Dame Paresseuse*, 1894, lithograph (W.62), 24 × 17 cm. Courtesy of the Trustees of the British Museum, London.

40: *The Siesta*, 1896, lithograph (W.122), 13.6 × 21 cm. Reproduced by courtesy of the Trustees of the British Museum, London.

41: *Firelight No. 2 – Joseph Pennell*, 1896, lithograph (W.105), 16.5 × 13 cm. Hunterian Art Gallery, University of Glasgow (Birnie Philip Bequest).

45: *Portrait of Whistler with Hat*, 1858, 46.3 × 38.1 cm. Freer Gallery of Art, Smithsonian Institution, Washington DC.

47: *Butcher's Shop, Saverne*, 1858, watercolour, 21.7 × 14.4 cm. Freer Gallery of Art, Smithsonian Institution, Washington DC.

49: *Harmony in Green and Rose: The Music Room*, 1860/61, 95.5 × 70.8 cm. Freer Gallery of Art, Smithsonian Institution, Washington DC.

51: *Blue and Silver: Blue Wave, Biarritz*, 1862, 61 × 87.6 cm. Hill-Stead Museum, Farmington, Connecticut.

53: *Wapping*, 1861–4, 71.1 × 101.6 cm. National Gallery of Art, Washington DC (John Hay Whitney Collection).

55: *Grey and Silver: Old Battersea Reach*, 1863, 49.5 × 67.9 cm. © 1990 The Art Institute of Chicago (Potter Palmer Collection 1922.449). All Rights Reserved.

57: *Symphony in White, No. 1: The White Girl*, 1862, 214.6 × 108 cm. National Gallery of Art, Washington DC (Harris Whittemore Collection).

59: *Caprice in Purple and Gold, No. 2: The Golden Screen*, 1864, 50.2 × 68.7 cm. Freer Gallery of Art, Smithsonian Institution, Washington DC.

61: *Symphony in White, No. 2: The Little White Girl*, 1864, 76 × 51 cm. Tate Gallery, London.

63: *Sea and Rain*, 1865, 50.8 × 72.7 cm. University of Michigan Museum of Art (Bequest of Margaret Watson Parker, 1955).

65: *Rose and Silver: The Princess from the Land of Porcelain*, 1863–4, 199.9 × 116.1 cm. Freer Gallery of Art, Smithsonian Institution, Washington DC.

67: *Symphony in Grey and Green: The Ocean*, 1866–72, 80.7 × 101.9 cm. Copyright the Frick Collection, New York.

69: *Symphony in White, No. 3*, 1865–7, 52 × 76.5 cm. The Barber Institute of Fine Arts, The University of Birmingham.

71: *The White Symphony: Three Girls*, 1868, 46.4 × 61.6 cm. Freer Gallery of Art, Smithsonian Institution, Washington DC.

73: *Variations in Flesh Colour and Green: The Balcony*, 1864–70, 61.4

× 48.8 cm. Freer Gallery of Art, Smithsonian Institution, Washington DC.

75: *Variations in Pink and Grey: Chelsea*, 1871/2, 62.7 × 40.5 cm. Freer Gallery of Art, Smithsonian Institution, Washington DC.

77: *Harmony in Grey and Green: Miss Cicely Alexander*, 1872–3, 190 × 98 cm. Tate Gallery, London.

79: *Nocturne in Blue and Silver*, 1871/2, 44.4 × 60.3 cm. Courtesy of the Fogg Art Museum, Harvard University, Cambridge, Massachusetts (Bequest of Grenville L. Winthrop).

81: *Arrangement in Grey and Black: Portrait of the Artist's Mother*, 1871, 144.3 × 165.2 cm. Musée du Louvre, Paris.

83: *Nocturne: Blue and Gold – Old Battersea Bridge*, 1872–3, 66.6 × 50.2 cm. Tate Gallery, London.

85: *Arrangement in Grey and Black, No. 2: Portrait of Thomas Carlyle*, 1872–3, 171 × 143.5 cm. Glasgow Art Gallery and Museum.

87: *Nocturne: Blue and Silver – Battersea Reach*, 1872/8, 39.4 × 62.9 cm. Isabella Stewart Gardner Museum, Boston (photo: Art Resource, New York).

89: *Maud Franklin*, c. 1875, 62.2 × 41 cm. Courtesy of the Fogg Art Museum, Harvard University, Cambridge, Massachusetts (Bequest of Grenville L. Winthrop).

91: *Nocturne: Grey and Gold – Westminster Bridge*, 1871/4, 47 × 62.3 cm. The Burrell Collection, Glasgow Museums and Art Galleries.

93: *Cremorne Gardens, No. 2*, 1875, 68.5 × 134.9 cm. Metropolitan Museum of Art, New York (John Stewart Kennedy Fund, 1912).

95: *Arrangement in Brown and Black: Miss Rosa Corder*, 1876–8, 192.4 × 92.4 cm. Copyright the Frick Collection, New York.

97: *Nocturne in Black and Gold: The Falling Rocket*, 1875, 60.3 × 46.6 cm. © The Detroit Institute of Arts (Gift of Dexter M. Ferry Jr).

99: *Arrangement in White and Black*, c. 1876, 191.4 × 90.9 cm. Freer Gallery of Art, Smithsonian Institution, Washington DC.

101: *Harmony in Blue: The Duet*, c. 1878, 27.3 × 45.7 cm. Museum of Art, Rhode Island School of Design, Providence, RI (Jesse Metcalfe Fund).

103: *The Gold Scab*, 1879, 186.7 × 137 cm. The Fine Arts Museums of San Francisco (Gift of Alma de Bretteville Spreckels through the Patrons of Art and Music).

105: *Winter Evening*, 1880, crayon and pastel, 30 × 20.2 cm. Freer Gallery of Art, Smithsonian Institution, Washington DC.

107: *Nocturne in Blue and Silver: The Lagoon, Venice*, 1879/80, 50.8 × 65.4 cm. Museum of Fine Arts, Boston (Emily L. Ainsley Fund).

109: *Arrangement in Black: The Lady in the Yellow Buskin – Portrait of Lady Archibald Campbell*, 1882–4, 213.3 × 109.2 cm. Philadelphia Museum of Art (W.P. Wilstach Collection).

111: *An Orange Note: Sweet Shop*, 1884, 12.2 × 21.5 cm. Freer Gallery of Art, Smithsonian Institution, Washington DC.

113: *Arrangement in Flesh Colour and Black: Portrait of Théodore Duret*, 1883–4, 193.4 × 90.8 cm. Metropolitan Museum of Art, New York (Catharine Lorillard Wolfe Collection 1913).

115: *Grey and Silver: Mist – Life Boat*, 1884, 12.3 × 21.6 cm. Freer Gallery of Art, Smithsonian Institution, Washington DC.

117: *White and Grey: The Hotel Courtyard, Dieppe*, 1885, 21.7 × 12.5 cm. Courtesy of the Fogg Art Museum, Harvard University, Cambridge, Massachusetts (Bequest of Grenville L. Winthrop).

119: *Blue and Violet: La Belle de Jour*, c. 1885, 17.2 × 10.8 cm. Courtesy of the Fogg Art Museum, Harvard University, Cambridge, Massachusetts (Bequest of Grenville L. Winthrop).

121: *Chelsea Shop*, 1887/90, 12.4 × 21.5 cm. Museum of Art, Rhode Island School of Design, Providence, RI.

123: *Harmony in Fawn Colour and Purple: Portrait of Miss Milly Finch*, c. 1885, 189.3 × 88.7 cm. Hunterian Art Gallery, University of Glasgow (Birnie Philip Gift).

125: *Flower Market, Dieppe*, 1885, watercolour, 12.8 × 21 cm. Freer Gallery of Art, Smithsonian Institution, Washington DC.

127: *London Bridge*, c. 1886, watercolour, 17.5 × 27.8 cm. Freer Gallery of Art, Smithsonian Institution, Washington DC.

129: *The Grey House*, 1889, 23.5 × 13.8 cm. Freer Gallery of Art, Smithsonian Institution, Washington DC.

131: *Annabel Lee*, c. 1890, crayon and pastel, 32.3 × 18 cm. Freer Gallery of Art, Smithsonian Institution, Washington DC.

133: *Arrangement in Flesh Colour and Brown: Portrait of Arthur J. Eddy*, 1894, 209.9 × 92.4 cm. © 1990 The Art Institute of Chicago (Arthur Jerome Eddy Memorial Collection 1931.501). All Rights Reserved.

135: *Miss Rosalind Birnie Philip Standing*, c. 1897, 23.4 × 13.7 cm. Hunterian Art Gallery, University of Glasgow (Birnie Philip Bequest).

137: *Portrait of Charles Lang Freer*, 1902, 51.8 × 31.7 cm. Freer Gallery of Art, Smithsonian Institution, Washington DC.

139: *Brown and Gold (Self-Portrait)*, 1895/1900, 95.8 × 51.5 cm. Hunterian Art Gallery, University of Glasgow (Birnie Philip Bequest).